# Inclusive High Schools

# Inclusive High Schools

## Learning from Contemporary Classrooms

by Douglas Fisher, Ph.D.,
Caren Sax, Ed.D., and Ian Pumpian, Ph.D.
Interwork Institute
San Diego State University

with invited contributors

·P·A·U·L·H·
BROOKES
PUBLISHING Co.

Baltimore · London · Toronto · Sydney

**Paul H. Brookes Publishing Co.**
Post Office Box 10624
Baltimore, Maryland 21285-0624

www.brookespublishing.com

Typeset by EvS Communication Networx, Point Pleasant, New Jersey.
Manufactured in the United States of America by
Versa Press, East Peoria, Illinois.

The names of the high schools discussed in this book have been changed to preserve the confidentiality of the high schools and the individuals associated with
them. For the same reason, teachers' affiliations and addresses have been omitted
from the authors' and contributors' listings at the front of this book. Readers who
wish to contact any of the authors or contributors may do so c/o Douglas Fisher,
Ph.D., Project Director, Interwork Institute, San Diego State University, 5850 Hardy
Avenue #112, San Diego, California 92182.

Permission to use the following is gratefully acknowledged:

Photographs copyright © 1999 by the University of New Hampshire, Durham.

Graphics/images on page 70, Figure 5, courtesy of ClickArt® Incredible Image
Pak™, copyright © 1996 The Learning Company, Inc., and its subsidiaries. All
rights reserved. Used by permission. ClickArt, Image Pak, and Brøderbund are
trademarks and/or registered trademarks of Learning Company Properties, Inc.

**Library of Congress Cataloging-in-Publication Data**

Inclusive high schools : learning from contemporary classrooms /
    [edited] by Douglas Fisher, Caren Sax, and Ian Pumpian.
        p.   cm.
    Includes bibliographical references (p.   ) and index.
    ISBN 1-55766-379-3
        1. Inclusive education—United States.   2. Exceptional children—
    Education (Secondary)—United States.   I. Fisher, Douglas.
    II. Sax, Caren.   III. Pumpian, Ian.
    LC1201.I539   1999
    371.9'Q473—dc21                                                    98-50819
                                                                            CIP

British Library Cataloguing in Publication data are available from the British
Library.

# Contents

# About the Authors

**Douglas Fisher, Ph.D.,** Assistant Professor and Project Director, has taught a range of courses in the teacher-credentialing program as well as graduate- and doctoral-level courses in the College of Education at San Diego State University (SDSU). He has served as a faculty member at Grossmont Community College, providing an important link between local high schools and SDSU. Through his position as Project Director at the Interwork Institute, Dr. Fisher has provided technical assistance and progressive preservice and in-service training to school districts, adult services agencies, and other community services providers in the areas of transition, curriculum development, policy change, assistive technology, and inclusive school reform.

**Caren Sax, Ed.D.,** Faculty Member and Project Director, has taught post-baccalaureate and graduate courses in the Department of Administration and Postsecondary Education, the Department of Special Education, and the School of Teacher Education at San Diego State University since 1990. She was a special education teacher in Arizona public schools for 15 years before joining the Interwork Institute. Her expertise includes assistive technology, teacher training, inclusive education, continuing education, transition from school to work, and distance learning.

**Ian Pumpian, Ph.D.,** Professor in Educational Leadership, has been a special education teacher, teacher educator, keynote speaker, and educational visionary. His expertise includes systems change efforts, school reform, and inclusive education.

# About the Contributors

**Eileen Bagg-Rizzo, M.A.,** Teacher, completed her master's degree at San Diego State University. Since 1986, she has been a general education English teacher in an inclusive high school in San Diego. Her interests include English education for all students, teacher mentoring, and differentiated instruction.

**Barbara Buswell, M.A.,** is Co-Director of the PEAK Parent Center, the federally funded Parent Training and Information Center in Colorado, and is the mother of Brook, Wilson, and Bronwen. Prior to creating PEAK, she was a high school English teacher. She has a master's degree in inclusive educational reform and is interested in the intersection of general and special education, especially with regard to standards and curriculum.

**Elizabeth Castagnera, M.A.,** Teacher, completed her master's degree at San Diego State University with an emphasis in special education. She is a high school teacher in San Diego, supporting students with disabilities in their general education classes. Her interests include curriculum development and modification, behavioral support strategies, and friendship facilitation.

**Lois Chappell, M.S.,** Teacher, has several credentials, including resource specialist, counselor, administrator, and teacher of students with mild disabilities. She has been a district resource specialist and a high school special education teacher. She serves as the Title I coordinator for a San Diego middle school and is an adjunct faculty member at San Diego State University. Her interests include school change, support for general education teachers, and literacy.

**Ronald James, Ph.D.,** Director of Research, earned his doctoral degree in organizational psychology from Purdue University. Since 1978, he has been involved in direct services, interdisciplinary training, and research focused on people with disabilities and their families. He has a strong professional and research background in interagency collaboration as well as the planning and direction of large-scale longitudinal studies. He has been actively engaged in coordinating program evaluation and research activities within the Center on Disability Studies (University Affiliated Program of Hawaii) since its inception. Dr. James has published in the areas of interagency planning and coordination, transition from school to adult environments, and family-driven services and supports. In addition, he has presented at numerous local, national, and international conferences.

**Cheryl M. Jorgensen, Ph.D.,** Research Associate Professor and Project Coordinator, has worked with New Hampshire schools since 1985 to help people in those schools increase their commitment and capacity to include students with disabilities in general education. Her expertise includes research, systems change, school reform, and inclusive high school education.

**Lyn Pratt,** Teacher, has taught high school students since 1995, playing a key role in promoting the inclusion of students with disabilities in general education classes. Along with her colleagues, she helped implement new strategies for infusing disability awareness activities throughout the curriculum.

**Virginia Roach, Ed.D.,** Deputy Executive Director, National Association of State Boards of Education (NASBE), is Co-Director of the Consortium on Inclusive Schooling Practices and of the Center for Policy Research on General and Special Education Reform, both of which are federally funded projects. She is the primary author of *Winners All: A Call for Inclusive Schools* (NASBE, 1992). Her interests include policy developments, linking policy with practice, and equity and excellence in public education.

**Karen Rodifer, M.A.,** Teacher, completed her master's degree with an emphasis in special education. She is a high school teacher in San Diego who supports students with disabilities in their general education classes. Her interests include schoolwide accommodations, peer tutoring, teacher development, and inclusive high school education.

**Garnett Smith, Ed.D.,** Associate Professor, earned his doctoral degree in special education at the University of Northern Colorado. He has served as an assistant professor in the Department of Special Education at the University of Hawaii at Manoa since 1990. He coordinated career transition programs at the University of South Alabama and was a member of the governor's task force on transition in the state of Alabama. Dr. Smith serves as the Special Needs Division Report Editor of *TECHniques* (formerly the *Vocational Education Journal* of the American Vocational Association). He has extensive research experience in transition and has written numerous publications and presentations in transition-related areas. He serves as a technical advisor to the Hawaii Interagency Transition Project and directs a project focused on the dissemination of effective transition practices.

**Robert Stodden, Ph.D.,** Director, has more than 25 years of experience as a secondary school teacher, teacher trainer, researcher, and writer in the field of secondary education and transition for youth with disabilities. He has served as Principal Investigator/Director for more than 50 research and systems development projects and has authored numerous books and journal articles in the field of special education. During the 1995–1996 academic year, Dr. Stodden served as a Kennedy Senior Policy Fellow in the U.S. Senate, negotiating and drafting much of the legislative language for the Individuals with Disabilities Education Act (IDEA) Amendments of 1997 (PL 105-17). He consults with several state departments of education on the implementation of IDEA requirements and regulations, especially those parts affecting youth with disabilities at the secondary school level.

**David Zaino, M.A.,** Teacher, completed his master's degree at San Diego State University with an emphasis in curriculum and instruction. He is a high school teacher in San Diego who supports students with disabilities in their general education classes. His interests include research on inclusive education, especially from students' perspectives; extracurricular activities for all students; and students' transitions to adult life.

# Foreword

There was something unique about the bus we were riding in on that cloudy, drizzly morning in March 1997. It was the peak of our trip to Washington, D.C., for Close-Up, and we were spending the day on Capitol Hill to meet our legislators. Dressed in tuxedos borrowed from Adam's Leaf, a tuxedo shop in Colorado Springs, Colorado, where we live, we were an unlikely pair: Aaron, the voluble one, and Wilson, who speaks without a voice and uses a wheelchair and a Canon communicator.

Our day on Capitol Hill was the most action packed, but the whole week was cool. Part of an amalgamation of more than 100 students from five states, we explored our nation's capitol, attended debates, visited historic sites and monuments, and became familiar with Washington as a community rather than as a shrine.

The group of students were divided into about 14 different groups called workshops. Our workshop was unique. Well, all high school students think they are unique; but our bus had a wheelchair lift. This provided students who did not have disabilities with the opportunity to learn more about and form friendships with students who happened to have a disability. That week, for us, a new adventure began. . . .

*Aaron:* Inside the Lincoln Memorial, standing in the exact spot where Martin Luther King, Jr., gave his "I Have a Dream" speech was the most memorable part of the trip for me.

*Wilson:* We all laughed at how I had the very same pose, in my wheelchair, as Abraham Lincoln had in his chair in the monument.

*Aaron:* I thought it was funny when we were in the basement of the Capitol, and the only potentially accessible rest room that we had found was a women's room. While you were in the rest room, I was guarding the doorway in my tuxedo. I felt like the Secret Service or one of Louis Farrakhan's bodyguards.

*Wilson:* Remember when we toured around inside the Capitol dome and we heard President Clinton was coming? Security was going to close off the Capitol, so we had to rush to get out of there and be on time to the bus. As we zipped from door to door following our instructor, it seemed that every exit had flights of stairs to get out.

*Aaron:* The subway from the Senate office building to the Capitol building was inaccessible. I remember telling the rest of our Close-Up group, "We'll beat you anyway," and we ran on the walkway next to the track and beat the subway and the Close-Up group to the Capitol.

*Wilson:* It was cool staying in the hotel, and because of the support I needed in the evenings, we were able to make our own curfew and cruise around after hours.

*Aaron:* I learned for the first time how well you can read with your peripheral vision during the liberal–conservative debate. I wrote, "Can you read this?" and you looked over and blinked. We then had a written conversation about the debate, and you gave a blink when I wrote, "Do you think she's cute?" I noticed that other kids were watching how we communicated during the debate—me writing questions, you blinking for yes or not blinking for no.

*Wilson:* Maybe they'll use my idea for passing notes in class.

Our week in Washington was busy. We learned many things about our government and its history. It was also a chance for us to teach others from around the United States about disability and inclusion. That one week in Washington, D.C., is a fraction of what happens in a fully inclusive educational environment.

When we were telling Douglas Fisher, Caren Sax, and Ian Pumpian about our trip, they told us about a book that they were working on. They said that there were a number of high schools across the United States that had changed and become inclusive. They asked us to consider writing the foreword for the book and to share our experiences and perspectives. They seemed to think that adults would be interested in the perspective of two high school seniors and their thoughts on friendship and inclusion. So, here goes.

## BECOMING FRIENDS

We were not paired as partners for a certain class; that is not how we became friends. We noticed each other in our junior year at Wasson High School. Both of us were fairly new; Wilson arrived in his junior year, and Aaron arrived in his sophomore year. We formally met in our senior year, when we were both involved in the Student Organization, which is the student council for our school.

*Aaron:* I wanted to get to know Wilson, but I didn't want Wilson to think I was being nice just to be nice or to look like one of those résumé-building teens who try to turn hanging out with someone as a friend into community service.

*Wilson:* I wanted to get to know Aaron but was kind of hesitant for a while, since he was the president of the student body.

The first week of class, Wilson was introduced to Aaron by a classmate named Jeremy. Jeremy found out from Jan Sutherland, one of our teachers, how Wilson communicated and what his talents, abilities, and interests were. It was an easy way for the class to learn how to talk with Wilson.

Each day in Student Organization, we would talk while making posters or get ideas from each other while brainstorming for new fund raisers or activities. Around Halloween, we knew that we both wanted to go on the Washington Close-Up trip. It took a while for us to know for sure if we could go. We had to overcome a couple of obstacles. The first was raising enough money for the trip, and the second was the attitudes and beliefs of some of the Close-Up staff. We heard that some staff members were skeptical about Wilson's support needs and questioned whether he should go. We made going to Washington, D.C., a priority, though, because we were eager to have our opinions about politics heard.

Planning the trip to D.C. helped us get to know each other outside of school as well. At basketball games, Aaron would embarrass Wilson with his obnoxiously loud comments about the other team. In class, Wilson would laugh at Aaron and make fun of him when he frantically searched for the agenda for the Student Organization meeting that day.

On our trip to D.C., we realized how alike we were, even though we had different opinions. We offered different perspectives to each other. Although we had differing political positions, with Wilson being the independent and Aaron being conservative, we respected each other because we are both fighters for social justice and believe in fighting the status quo. We both communicate a lot through our actions.

We became friends because of all of the experiences we have had together: the experiences in Washington and the experiences at basketball games outside school, and our experiences in the community discussions on racism. Our friendship had to begin in a general education classroom, though. When we read the book you are about to read, we learned that lots of people share our experiences. It comes down to one thing: You have to be there.

## UNDERSTANDING FRIENDSHIP

"How's Wilson? Has he urinated yet?" asked the nurse. The only way I could respond was by saying, "I don't know. May I take a message and have his parents call you?" Aaron reports. What a crazy conversation. Nobody would call and ask my friends that, I hope!

Everywhere we go, it is assumed that, since we are hanging out together, we must be brothers or else Aaron is an aide and has expertise with Wilson's medical needs. In D.C., Aaron told at least six people that we were not brothers. When I got tight sitting in my wheelchair for a long time, people even asked Aaron, "Who taught you how to rub Wilson's shoulders?"

One girl came up to us and said, "That's so great that you're helping him out." She had good intentions, but it still angered Aaron. She did not have a clue. Helpers are teens who join some school program working with certain students for part of a class to add to their community service list. Wilson cannot stand people who are acting as helpers at least partly for selfish reasons. If that girl had truly experienced inclusion, she would have congratulated Wilson for helping me to understand the range of human experience, the more liberal side of politics, and how to drive a van! Until inclusive education, especially in the high school, becomes more common, people will continue to misunderstand friendship.

## NEEDED CHANGES

Wilson enjoyed his last few years in high school. He was able to get involved in Student Organization; take advanced classes in English, math, and the sciences; and kick back and enjoy basketball games. It was an amazing experience for both of us. We just needed a chance to get to know each other. How can society expect us to accept people with disabilities if we are taught in separate classrooms or treated like we should be separated?

ACT did a study to find out what was the number 1 factor in determining future success. That factor was involvement in extracurricular activities because in that aspect of their high school experience, students learned how to work with people with different personalities and egos. The reason why some people with disabilities do not succeed later in life is the same reason why people without disabilities do not succeed later in life. It is not because they have not learned job skills but rather because they have not learned how to deal effectively with people.

American society is still backward in the way it deals with people who have disabilities and with people who are different in general. It seems ironic that the one subway that led directly underneath the Capitol was inaccessible—Capitol Hill, the place that is supposed to provide the moral leadership, believe it or not, for the United States. Congress passes legislation like the Americans with Disabilities Act (ADA) of 1990 (PL 101-336), but what really needs to change is Americans' attitudes toward people who have disabilities. Attitudes like the ones that kept Wilson from being able to join the Student Council at a previous high school. Attitudes like the ones some of the teachers had that kept Wilson from joining group activities with the other students—segregation. Attitudes of college admissions directors who refused to admit Wilson because they did not think his intelligence could accurately be measured—scared. Attitudes assuming that we are brothers—traditional pity.

*Aaron:* When one person asked if we were brothers, I responded sarcastically, "Why the hell would I wanna be related to *him*?" Wilson responded with a strong blink, meaning, "Ditto." The person walked away and left us alone.

*Wilson:* The nurse's question to Aaron when he answered the telephone wasn't mean or ignorant; it was just habit. I need support for things like taking medicine, eating through my g-tube, getting in and out of my wheelchair, and breathing treatments. This means that people like nurses are in my life each day. It's only a small part of my life, though.

*Aaron:* Through an inclusive educational philosophy at Wasson, Wilson has been able to show other students his personality and abilities. Wasson's principal, Jackie Provenzano, describes Wilson as "a teacher to teachers." He has made many real friends. The nurse just happened to call while we were hanging out. Maybe I should have explained to her that guys keep track of each other's urinary habits only when we are in the woods having a contest to see who can do it the farthest.

Although we have been able to share some cool and crazy experiences, we know that there are schools out there that follow a noninclusive philosophy. Students are left in "special" classrooms and live around only other people who have disabilities. Aaron has made it clear that he would hate a school with only European American males who communicated in the same way he does. Part of the excitement of our world is the diversity that we all get to experience.

A girl named Natalie who was in our Close-Up workshop in Washington sent Wilson a postcard. It reads, "I just wanted to let you know how cool it was to have you in the workshop I was in. I hope you had as much fun as I did. I had so many stories to tell when I got home, and without the diversity of students who were there, I don't think I would have had as many."

Our friend Freddie said he knew a kid in Hawaii who had a disability like Wilson's and even the Deep South country boys from Alabama in our group could relate to disability. Maybe just as the trip to D.C. made a difference in their lives, our other friends from Alabama, Colorado, Hawaii, Massachusetts, and Michigan all have stories to tell and friendships to begin.

We think that you will see a lot of examples of what can change in high school by reading this book.

*Aaron:* Can you believe it? We get to assign reading to adults, a lot of them teachers!

*Wilson:* Yes, maybe we should have a test at the end. Of course, our test wouldn't be multiple-choice or true-false. Our test would be one of those fancy school-to-career versions: Can they use what they have learned?

*Aaron and Wilson:* Time to do your homework!

*Wilson Buswell and Aaron Flint*
*Wasson High School, Class of 1998*

# To Our Readers

We have been friends, colleagues, and collaborators in our exploration of school restructuring, inclusive education, teacher preparation, and learning how all the pieces fit together. Our journeys have sometimes been on the same path; yet each of us has taken detours, meeting again at another point down the road. We have each experienced working in segregated environments designed for people with disabilities and felt the frustration of coping with large bureaucracies as we pushed for change. Since we have joined forces at San Diego State University, we have continued our mutual quest to push the boundaries. We have learned to listen more effectively to people with disabilities and their families and friends, as well as to teachers, administrators, and community members, in order to help design and promote the best education possible for all students. The more we learn, the more we realize that we still have a long way to go.

In brainstorming the underlying ideas and format of this book, we found that it seemed to take on a life of its own. The book evolved as our understanding of the issues broadened, and our understanding of the issues broadened as we added more perspectives. In our attempt to provide stories of schools that each began at different points and progressed at different rates, we realized that each scenario had unique lessons to offer. As we asked our colleagues to read and react to the school case studies and to provide their unique perspectives, we learned even greater lessons. We hope that teachers, administrators, family members, and related support staff find useful information and strategies that can be put into practice immediately. We also hope that they use these lessons that we have learned as a catalyst for more dialogue about what is possible in their own schools and communities. Join us as we continue to learn from one another.

# Acknowledgments

Thanking all of those responsible for making this book a reality is no easy task. Working as a team prevents anyone from truly owning an idea or an innovation. We build on one another's ideas; brainstorm to increasingly more complex levels; and look to our colleagues for support, constructive criticism, and brutal honesty.

We would first like to acknowledge our editors at Brookes, Scott Beeler and Lisa Benson, for believing in us and our ideas and guiding us through the publication process. After we had their support, we turned to the teachers, administrators, and students at the schools with which we have worked most closely. Being able to step back to gain perspective and chronicle years of change is often difficult. The high school teachers who contributed to this book—Eileen Bagg-Rizzo, Liz Castegnera, Lois Chappell, Lyn Pratt, Karen Rodifer, and David Zaino—are phenomenal role models, teacher-leaders, and catalysts for change in their schools. They, along with their colleagues, have pushed the boundaries for creating more inclusive schools. Of course, we must thank all of the students who keep us grounded in what works and what needs to be changed in classrooms.

We would also like to thank each of our other contributors, who offered insightful perspectives that added greater breadth and depth to the book. Each has his or her own unique manner of examining an issue, analyzing its impact, and eloquently summarizing the next steps toward change. The contributors have added a great deal to this book. Cheryl M. Jorgensen of the Institute on Disability at the University of New Hampshire deserves special note. Her insightful and probing questions as well as the friendship that has developed between us are reflected throughout this book.

We would like to give special thanks to Wilson Buswell and Aaron Flint, who wrote the foreword for this book from their unique positions as graduating high school seniors. They see the world as it can be and will certainly continue to make an impact on everyone they meet. In addition, the photographers who were able to capture our words with pictures—John Graham, Chris Jones, Gary Sampson (Institute on Disability at the University of New Hampshire), and David Zaino—have clearly left their marks in these pages.

Finally, we would like to thank our families for their patience and support during the deadline crunches and the hours of writing and agonizing over details. We are extremely fortunate to have such unconditional love.

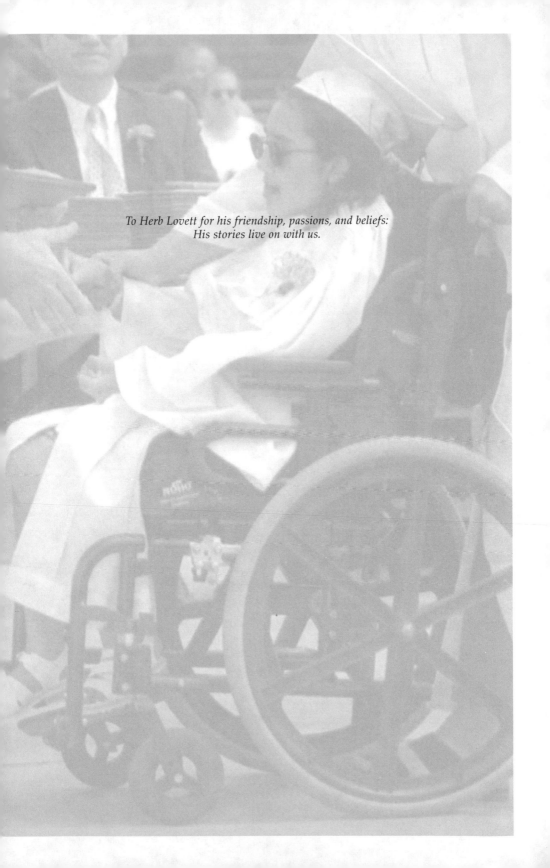

*To Herb Lovett for his friendship, passions, and beliefs:*
*His stories live on with us.*

# Inclusive High Schools

1

# We Had to
# See it for Ourselves

An Introduction to Inclusive High Schools

Douglas Fisher
Ian Pumpian
Caren Sax

This book is about high schools that have changed the way in which supports and services are provided to all students and about the people who have made these changes happen. The reflections of teachers and the case studies of schools in this book were selected with the intention of providing a range of demographic information about inclusive education. Both general and special educators' voices are represented in this book, as are rural and urban schools, small and large schools, and schools with diverse student populations. The teachers and schools featured in this book were also purposely selected to demonstrate some of the different ways in which systems evolve to become more inclusive. Demetra Jackson of John Q. Adams High School (see also Chapter 6) reported to the authors that

> We first got together and talked about inclusive education for all students when we were awarded the Research, Development and Demonstration grant from the state [Department of Education]. We had been providing mainstreaming and inclusive experiences for students with mild disabilities for several years, but students with more severe disabilities were often not part of our efforts. Now, don't get me wrong, we had a few parents that advocated on behalf of their children to be in regular classes, and we always accommodated individual requests. For the most part, our program for students with severe disabilities was significantly more community based and vocationally oriented.

Each chapter makes a unique contribution to the book. Taken together, they provide credible evidence to support inclusive education and the need for restructuring at the secondary school level. Each chapter in this book provides several concepts to consider with regard to the relationship between inclusive education and high school restructuring.

Chapter 2 identifies eight themes of general education reform and how these reforms affect students with disabilities. In addition, it provides an overview of change models and the ways in which schools have begun to implement inclusive, restructuring efforts. This framework is presented to provide a context for the other chapters in the book.

Chapters 3 and 4 provide personal accounts of changes in practice from the perspectives of a special educator and a general educator, respectively. Chapters 5–7 provide case studies of three high schools that have undergone changes to implement inclusive education. The remainder of the book provides reflections on these personal accounts and case studies from policy makers, educators, and parents.

In Chapter 3, David Zaino, a high school special education teacher, discusses his personal and professional changes of opinion about inclusive education. He relates a compelling story about a student named Christina and her journey from a Romanian orphanage to an inclusive American high school. In addition, he provides an analysis of the current research on inclusive education. Through his discussion of Christina and his analysis of changes in the field of special education, he shares his own personal and professional journey. This journey has taken him from being a staff member in a sheltered workshop for transition-age students to becoming a valued member of a comprehensive high school.

In Chapter 4, Eileen Bagg-Rizzo, a high school English teacher, paints a different picture of inclusion for us. She discusses a student with an individualized education program (IEP) and the changes in that student's educational goals as she moved from a segregated junior high school to an inclusive high school. Bagg-Rizzo also writes of her own educational experiences and the absence of individuals with disabilities in her own life. Similar to Zaino's reflections, Bagg-Rizzo's describe her own growth from working as a content specialist prepared to teach a select group of high achievers to working as a teacher prepared to set high expectations for achievement among all learners.

In Chapter 5, two high school teachers, Karen Rodifer and Elizabeth Castagnera, discuss the changes at their school. Their high school case study combines a case-by-case approach to inclusive education with whole-school change. In addition, their chapter covers block scheduling, senior projects, and curriculum modifications.

In Chapter 6, Lois Chappell, a vice principal, and Lyn Pratt, a high school special education teacher, explain the change that their school experienced in moving toward inclusive education. Their high school case study illustrates how a state-funded pilot project facilitated whole-school change. A number of activities that have been used at their school to introduce diversity and disability into content-area classes are explained. These activities provide teachers with ways to enter the inclusion conversation with their students.

In Chapter 7, Cheryl M. Jorgensen, a research associate professor at the Institute on Disability at the University of New Hampshire, provides an overview of the opening of a new, inclusive high school. Her case study examines a phased-in approach to whole-school change. She allows readers an inside look at the way in which a school's operating principles can create an inclusive agenda. She offers a glimpse at the operation of the school by explaining how teachers create inclusive lessons. Her chapter also covers new uses of time, critical friends, and governance structures in an inclusive secondary school environment.

The authors of Chapters 8–11 discuss the personal reflections and case studies presented in Chapters 2–7. Reflections on those previous chapters are provided from the perspective of change theory and inclusive education (Chapter 8); policy, achievement, and inclusive education (Chapter 9); personnel development and inclusive practices (Chapter 10); and parent involvement in educational efforts (Chapter 11). In Chapter 8, colleagues from the University of Hawaii—Garnett Smith, Robert Stodden, and Ronald James—join in reflecting on the changes that teachers and schools experienced. They propose a framework for considering and understanding school change. In Chapter 9, Virginia Roach provides another analysis of the teacher and school changes presented in the case studies in this book. She examines these changes from the perspective of policy analysis and identifies three components of student achievement that must be addressed: curriculum, instruction, and placement. In Chapter 10, Ian Pumpian discusses the need for a change in teacher education practices and policies. His analysis of the need for a comprehensive system of professional development indicates that training programs must be aligned with the outcomes that school administrators and educators seek, and he proposes a way to achieve that goal. In Chapter 11, Barbara Buswell, a parent and Co-Director of the PEAK Parent Center, reminds readers of the role that parents continue to play in education. She also challenges readers to consider another need: continuity, a theme that provides a suitable conclusion for the book. Buswell believes that parents and educators must become responsible for learning about effective practices to be implemented with students with and without disabilities and relaying that information to teachers and students because without continuity, parents and educators just keep starting over again and again in trying new practices.

# We Didn't Always Learn What We Were Taught....

## Inclusion *Does* Work!

Caren Sax
Douglas Fisher
Ian Pumpian

The culture of what is known as *special education* has changed dramatically since the 1960s. We began our special education careers working in institutions specifically designed to "care-take" people with disabilities. In these direct care positions, we experienced firsthand the most restrictive environment in the continuum of placements (see also Deno, 1970). Since those early days, each of us has struggled with the attitudes, expectations, and ethical questions associated with providing supports, services, and education to people with disabilities. As we became teachers and then teacher educators, we came to the conclusion that we could not expect to teach wise practices without providing an understanding of the concepts, theories, and metaphors that were handed down to us by our predecessors. Our experiences with students and families continue to confirm our belief in the value of inclusive communities and schools.

In the early 1990s, we met Peyton, who had just enrolled in a public high school. Prior to that, she had been in segregated schooling for several years of her life. It has taken us years to understand the impact on her of her removal from the learning community. If the isolation that Peyton and her family experienced had continued, hundreds of high school students would also have missed the opportunity to meet her. In fact, they almost did miss out on meeting her. The students who know her tell us how she has significantly influenced their attitudes, expectations, and understanding of people with disabilities. She is no longer in danger of being mistreated or marginalized. We are cognizant and concerned that, depending on how we structure schooling, we risk cheating the next generation of these experiences. The movement that we and Peyton experienced through the continuum of placements has convinced each of us that the placement continuum model hinders educational progress. We have also come to believe that we have new lessons to learn and expectations to develop as we make our schools and communities more inclusive.

As we reflect on our experiences with Peyton and compare them with our own early experiences and introductions to disability and society's expectations for people with disabilities, we wonder why we did not accept the way things were. All of our lives we have been sent powerful messages influencing our attitudes and expectations; only in the 1990s have the messages reinforced a new set of values. Thankfully, the lessons that we were taught were not always the same as those that we learned. The following poem expresses how our attitudes and expectations have changed.

### We didn't always learn what we were taught. . . .

*We were taught . . .*
   *People with medical conditions needed their own islands.*
*We learned . . .*
   *No one is an island.*

*We were taught . . .*
   *It's not polite to stare.*
*We learned . . .*
   *"Look at me now!"*

*We were taught . . .*
   *Adults with disabilities need day care.*
*We learned . . .*
   *Co-workers care.*

*We were taught . . .*
   *Wheelchairs confine.*
*We learned . . .*
   *If you can't stand up, stand out!*

*We were taught . . .*
   *People could be warehoused.*
*We learned . . .*
   *People need keys to their own house.*

*We were taught . . .*
   *Professionals have all the answers.*
*We learned . . .*
   *Families still had questions.*

*We were taught . . .*
   *General and special educators didn't need to talk.*
*We learned . . .*
   *"Can we talk!"*

*We were taught . . .*
   *Students with disabilities need to be with their own kind.*
*We learned . . .*
   *Students are kind to one another,*

*And that . . .*
  *Students come in all kinds.*

*We were taught . . .*
  *It takes a special person.*
*We learned . . .*
  *That it does.*
*And we're still learning. . . .*

Imagine the visual images that accompany the stanzas of the poem. Switch back and forth in your mind between stark, black-and-white images of the institutions that formerly housed people with disabilities and colorful images featuring people with disabilities and their friends and families participating in all facets of life. Those who have always believed it takes special people to support people with disabilities were right. We initially thought, however, that we could simply "manufacture" special people and then send people with disabilities to them. We were looking in the wrong places. As it turns out, special people are universal—people with disabilities need the same unique combination of friends, family, community members, and competent professionals that all human beings need to learn and thrive.

Many social changes have occurred in a relatively short time, and people with disabilities and their families have forged the way to discovering new opportunities beyond institutional walls. By working and living in our community's schools and neighborhoods, people with disabilities are no longer isolated. They, along with the professionals with whom they work, continue to demonstrate to the rest of society that everyone benefits when tolerance and acceptance head the list of priorities for how to live in diverse communities. Americans live in a diverse society that embraces democratic values. Schools have some responsibility to prepare students to understand, value, and develop comfort and competence in interacting with each other and understanding each other's differences. Teachers who did not experience this diversity in their own preparation often find it difficult to teach what they have not learned and experience difficulty when expected to foster inclusive attitudes concerning people with disabilities.

Despite the challenges and the lingering messages of the past, growing numbers of teachers, parents, and students are involved in successful inclusive educational experiences. With these experiences, particularly those linked to school restructuring initiatives that demonstrate better education for all students, new questions are being asked. Instead of people asking "Should we do it?" more are asking "How will we do it better?" Teachers, administrators, families, students, and community members are providing new answers to the second question, many of which are highlighted in this book. Every school finds answers differently, at different paces, and with different results. In this book, we describe the journeys that two teachers (see Chapters 3 and 4) and three schools (see Chapters 5–7) took and are still taking toward creating an inclusive educational experience. Inclusive education, like all education, is a process. In this chapter, we draw from the literature on school restructuring and inclusive education to define inclusive, restructuring schools; provide a context for understanding school change; and describe a framework for initiating school change efforts.

## INCLUSIVE, RESTRUCTURING SCHOOLS

The National Association of State Boards of Education (NASBE) Study Group on Special Education described inclusive education as follows:

> At its core, inclusion means that students attend their home school along with their age and grade peers. A truly inclusive schooling environment is one in which students with the full range of abilities and disabilities receive their in-school educational services in the general education classroom with appropriate in-class support. In an inclusive education system, the proportion of students labeled for special services is relatively uniform for the schools within a particular school district and reflects the proportion of people with disabilities in society at large. In short, inclusion is not a place or a method of delivering instruction; it is a philosophy of supporting children in their learning that undergirds the entire system. It is part of the very culture of a school or school district and defines how students, teachers, administrators, and others view the potential of children. The inclusive philosophy of supported education espoused is truly grounded in the belief that all children can learn and achieve. (1995, p. 4)

Implementation of special education legislation (the Individuals with Disabilities Education Act [IDEA] of 1990 [PL 101-476] and its 1991 [PL 102-119] and 1997 [PL 105-17] amendments) continues to result in the placement of large numbers of children with identified special education and related-services needs in environments other than the general education classroom. IDEA does contain an expectation that educational placement outside the general education program be provided when necessary. It qualifies its continuum provisions, however, by requiring that children be placed in the general educational environment unless the school or institution can demonstrate that the education of the individual student with a disability cannot "with the use of supplementary aids and service be achieved satisfactorily" (20 U.S.C. § 1412[5][B]).

Experience throughout the world suggests that we have just scratched the surface of what sorts of accommodations and adaptations are possible within the general education program. Therefore, as knowledge and experiences accrue, placements outside the general education program should rapidly fade. Unfortunately, segregated placements persist despite the range of information available to state and local programs on how to develop inclusive educational opportunities (e.g., NASBE, 1992; Stainback, Stainback, & Forest, 1989; Villa, Thousand, Stainback, & Stainback, 1992). Without question, the context of education reform can and should provide new opportunities to explore ways in which the general education program can be rich and flexible enough to accommodate the unique needs of each learner.

Service delivery systems are changing significantly. When inclusive education occurs in a restructuring school, the importance of overall school reform efforts must be recognized. A national outcry in support of efficient and effective schools that meet the needs of all students is under way (Sizer, 1992; Wilson & Daviss, 1994). At least eight themes seem to be consistent across the educational reform literature. Each of the following themes is described here and applied to creating inclusive school communities:

- School-site management
- Leadership style
- School stability
- Curriculum organization
- Staff development needs
- Establishing and supporting the active roles of parents
- Maximizing and recognizing academic success
- Community involvement

## Theme 1: School-Site Management

Responsibility for making decisions about mission, management, structure, and programs can no longer be outside the purview of the school's students, parents, teachers, administrators, and community members (General Accounting Office, 1994; Glickman, 1993; Oakes & Lipton, 1990; Patterson, Purkey, & Parker, 1986). Site-based management teams and processes are responsible for the look, feel, and mission of the school. Stakeholders maintain a dialogue among their constituency and bring unique and common concerns to the attention of the site-based teams. Input from stakeholders and stakeholder groups is democratically considered when allocating resources, distributing funds, and planning the physical and social environment of the school (Sergiovanni, 1996; Wohlstetter, Smyer, & Mohrman, 1994).

> **To achieve** a truly inclusive school community, all stakeholders need to have a voice in planning and implementing new directions.

## Theme 2: Leadership Style

If schools are to be the critical and inquiring communities necessary in a democratic society, then the leadership within them needs to conduct its affairs educationally and pedagogically instead of in a bureaucratic and authoritarian manner (Smyth, 1988). Leaders within the model inclusive school should be closely involved and connected to the site-based team. All members of the organization should have the capacity and the opportunity to be leaders (Wohlstetter et al., 1994). Would-be leaders should understand the world within and beyond the organization and develop a vision for the organization's future (Patterson et al., 1986).

> **To achieve** a truly inclusive school community, it is critical that a new belief system and vision for education that includes all students be created through leadership that focuses on building consensus through collaborative planning and that also clearly articulates goals for all students and the changes needed to meet those goals (NASBE, 1992).

## Theme 3: School Stability

Certainly, many outside factors influence the transfer rate of students and teachers, especially in inner-city communities. Several factors inherent in the school's structure, however, can promote stability. Small schools, schools within schools, families of classrooms, multi-age looping, alternative scheduling, mentoring programs, internships, service learning, and new school facility designs have been promoted as means of creating school stability by increasing relationships and time shared between adults and students. For teachers, these factors also include an increase in autonomy, influence on policy and curriculum, a reduction in noninstructional tasks, and provision for professional levels of working conditions and salaries (Feinberg & Soltis, 1992; Sizer, 1992). Moreover, collegial authority, facilitation of collaborative teaming, and decision-making structures help to create a supportive atmosphere for instruction staff. The theory is that if a school becomes a learning community, then good teachers will want to stay and teaching and learning will improve. Teachers will learn to recognize each other's skills and talents and to negotiate new working relationships (NASBE, 1992; Sailor, 1991). Specialists and generalists will work together to support broadly the needs of the entire school.

Theoretically, parents will work harder to keep their children attending a school that they believe is an inviting place; is reaching out to its community; and is caring toward, committed to, and effective for their children. Furthermore, when students experience responsibility, independence, collaboration, and group and personal fulfillment, their desire to remain at their school is enhanced. Students' opportunities to teach and learn, to determine accommodations and instructional adaptations, to serve as advocates for themselves and other students, and to provide social supports to others are important parts of their growing commitment to their school and its stability. They should also be a part of the governance structure of their schools and serve as members of school committees (Thousand & Villa, 1992). Empowering students and reaffirming their place in schools also influences their academic, social, emotional, personal, and collective responsibility and leadership development (NASBE, 1992). Children need the opportunity to experience and create social connections in school, and they need schools that facilitate this process (Kuhmerker, 1992). Too many people fail to see that students' working together and developing friendships are important functions and outcomes for schools; as a result, schools frequently neglect this area.

> **To achieve** a truly inclusive school community, a climate in which there is empathy, respect, and friendship among students and staff is needed to intentionally increase the security and stability of school "life" and the student body.

## Theme 4: Curriculum Organization

The challenge to a modern, diverse school is to develop a curriculum that is multilingual, multicultural, and option filled (Darder, 1991). Modifying instruction practices to include cooperative learning, activity-based and experiential instruction, and brain-based activities introduces strategies that may be more effective for more students than other strategies (e.g., Christ, 1995; Jensen, 1998). Teachers who are engaged in curriculum mapping (Jacobs, 1997) and similar processes are exploring ways to improve teaching and learning by aligning curriculum, building interdisciplinary units, and constructing lessons around essential questions. Schools can propose a flexible distribution of classes based on individual interests and needs because traditional models (which require strict adherence to graduation requirements) are contributing to the number of dropouts. The efficacy of curriculum flexibility is not a new finding (Dewey, 1916). An 8-year study conducted in the 1930s (*Adventures in American Education Series,* 1942, cited in Glines, 1984) concluded that students can experience success in college and adult life without following a standard curriculum. Postman, Sizer, Meir, and other leading reformers and theorists continue to argue for greater flexibility and depth in curriculum. Nonetheless, the reliance on the textbook as a bible and on standardized assessment as gospel continues. Without following a standard curriculum, the inclusion of students with severe disabilities often exposes a failure to establish a flexible curriculum structure and underscores the need to attend to diversity. In addition, schoolwide support for a flexible curriculum requires attention to new teaching strategies and more authentic assessment and exhibitions of learning (Cummins, 1989).

> To achieve a truly inclusive school community, curriculum must be flexible, must be responsive to students' strengths and needs, must include opportunities for cooperative learning and experiential activities, and must allow for individualized and authentic learning.

## Theme 5: Staff Development Needs

Schools using site-based management often create committees to conduct routine needs assessments (Feinberg & Soltis, 1992). These groups then guide the design of staff development activities. Staff development is generally more accepted when it is organized and conducted primarily by members of the community that the school serves (Stolovitch & Lane, 1989). Professionals also are more responsible when information is made available to them so that they can make informed decisions (Sergiovanni, 1996). Teachers need information; time to discuss, reflect, and plan together; and more time to work together in cooperative groups to train, coach, and mentor each other. Training should be supported by many follow-up activities, planning time, and access to technical assistance and resources (Servatius, Fellows, & Kelly, 1989).

Schools should limit the practice of dividing staff by specialty and discipline for the purpose of staff development. Although these divisions are sometimes necessary, other development activities should be designed to help teachers learn to bring their expectations to a team and schoolwide process. Individualized training plans for new teachers can be developed via a teacher support team model. Support teams can assist new teachers to create an individualized action plan based on individual teachers' specific interests and training needs. Staff development activities should be designed to attain schoolwide goals and address school priorities. Evidence of the effectiveness of this approach to staff development can come from observations; evaluations; and the performance of teachers, parents, and students.

To achieve a truly inclusive school community, staff development activities need to be responsive to teachers' interests and based on a collaborative approach. A separate agenda for general education and special education staff development should be avoided. Teaching and learning for a diverse student population should be a focus of staff development.

## Theme 6: Establishing and Supporting the Active Roles of Parents

Parents need to be welcomed as partners in the education of their children (Tucker et al., 1995). Their participation in school activities such as homework, sports events, and attendance is likely to influence student performance and increase motivation (Hickman, Greenwood, & Miller, 1995). According to Epstein, "When parents and teachers share instructional responsibilities, homes become more school like, and schools become more family like" (as cited in Oakes & Lipton, 1990, p. 16). As a result, these two complementary environments help the student develop academically, socially, and personally.

To promote parent involvement in school activities, schools can provide family seminars with flexible hours, child care options, and easy access to useful materials relevant to their children's success in school. Schools clearly need to be a part of parent education, volunteer coordination, and job development activities in communities challenged by poverty conditions (Epstein, 1995). These are crucial components of parent/guardian involvement, given the dramatic changes in family structures since the 1960s. For example, in 1992, Hanson and Lynch found that only 28% of students lived with both biological parents, which was down from 75% in 1960. In California, for every two public school children who spoke English at home, one child's primary language was not English. More than 1 million students in California have been classified as English language learners (Lara, 1994). This change in student demographics requires that school staff and counselors be sensitive to differences when implementing family involvement programs (Baruth & Manning, 1991). Haycock and Navarro's (1988) work reinforced the need to support and commit resources to family involvement. These authors, however, described the barriers to this goal that socioeconomic factors pose:

> Virtually all parents want the same thing for their children: a college education and a happy, productive life. But when it comes to translating these aspirations into day-to-day practices, well-educated parents have an advantage: they know what makes a difference. These days, it's hard for most parents to devote a lot of attention to their children's education. (1988, p. 22)

Educators need to bring family members together in creative ways and determine methods of securing their ongoing involvement. Person-centered planning and family involvement are key to the success of these efforts. Reformed schools often support parents and caregivers to function in mentor roles with other parents, thus enabling linguistic and ethnic matches among parents supporting each other and ensuring the relevance of school–parent participation programs.

---

**To achieve** a truly inclusive school community, families must be supported to provide input and be actively involved in planning for their children's education programs and future goals. Special educators who play critical instructional and supportive roles must collaborate with their instruction teams and make a place at the table for parents and students.

---

## Theme 7: Maximizing and Recognizing Academic Success

Learning time can be maximized by involving parents, empowering students, and allocating resources for individualized instruction (Fisher, Sax, & Pumpian, 1996). Recognition of success based on individual measures of growth and progress will particularly benefit students who, in the past, may have been relegated to low-status positions in the school. Recognition should also highlight positive examples of cooperation and collaboration among students and staff alike (Putnam, 1998). In addition to the core curriculum and the flexible programs available, schools should have supplemental resources to meet the unique needs of their culturally rich populations (Darder, 1991). For example, one student may develop goals that enable him or her to attend a university with an emphasis in drama. While designing his or her program, this student may use additional resources that will allow the student to maintain his or her native language while strengthening English language skills (Cummins, 1989; Ochoa & Romo, 1977).

As the school seeks to function as a center for community activity, the curriculum may be expanded to include the surrounding community and neighborhood as an extension of the learning environment. Development of a curriculum rich in community partnerships ensures communication and collaboration with local businesses, organizations, and key community leaders. Furthermore, many educators believe that not all learning takes place at the school site (Christ, 1995). Therefore, supplemental out-of-school educational experiences and opportunities could or should be provided by establishing partnerships with the business community and by involving students in community service projects (Massachusetts Institute of Technology, Quality Education for Minorities Project, 1990). A redefinition of *the classroom* needs to be developed. Again, this is an area where specialized staff (e.g., special educators, aides, speech-language therapists) will provide a great resource in the development and implementation of community-based curriculums and programs (Sailor, 1991).

> **To achieve** a truly inclusive school community, academic success must be determined on an individual basis and celebrated at a school–community level. To accomplish this goal, other adults need to accept roles as teaching mentors, and students need to learn and apply their learning to the community at large.

## Theme 8: Community Involvement

Effective reform needs to be based on the notion that trust and confidence arise when people believe that they can count on coherence, competence, and integrity from their peers (Patterson et al., 1986). Teachers across the United States have been extremely influential in supporting students with and without disabilities in developing social networks. Individuals who have been disconnected or disenfranchised often need the support of a facilitator (i.e., community connector) to help establish a circle of friends and a bridge to their community. A circle of friends, or personal support network, can

18     Sax, Fisher, and Pumpian

function as that bridge. Villa and Thousand described the importance of a social network or circle of friends as follows:

> The 21st century . . . will be a rapidly changing, information-based, communication-dependent, interdependent, world-wide marketplace that will require problem solving, human interaction, self-education, and self-discipline skills of its workers. For our children to survive as workers, their educational experiences must be quite different from those of the tribal, factory, or hospital models of schooling. Their schooling must not only give them practice in expending mental effort and taking charge of their own learning, but must model the equity and parity they will be expected to demonstrate with future co-workers of diverse skills, backgrounds, cultures, and values. (1992, p. 111)

---

**To achieve** a truly inclusive school community, the educational community not only must focus on improved student outcomes but also must build trust and confidence among its members. A democratic society depends on members who act not only in their own self-interest but also in the interest of others—that is, for the common good.

---

## FROM IDEAS TO IMPLEMENTATION

Although the eight themes just discussed provide a foundation for thinking about inclusive schools, their value can be realized only through implementation. Teachers and teacher educators representing a number of school districts across the United States compared notes regarding their change efforts. The conversation focused on specific practices that support students with disabilities to be educated alongside their peers. Eight practices of inclusive, restructuring schools were identified (see Fisher, Sax, & Jorgensen, 1998, pp. 31–32). Table 1 describes these practices, which are used throughout the remainder of the chapter as a starting point for discussing how schools change to become more inclusive.

### Change as a Process

"We say that people innately resist change. But the resistance we experience from others is not to change itself. It is to the particular process of change that believes in imposition rather than creation" (Wheatley & Kellner-Rogers, 1996, p. 99). Stated more simply, people

Table 1.    Principles of inclusive, restructuring schools

1.  Decisions about inclusive education and school reform must originate in administrative vision that is unwavering in the face of uncertainty and the difficulties of putting principles into practice.
2.  Inclusion of students with disabilities must be based solidly within general education reform efforts.
3.  Support for teachers and administrators during the change process must be provided through internal structures and through the association with an outside critical friend. Critical friends are often individuals from universities or funded agencies. These individuals have relationships with teachers in the school and provide resources, ask hard program-related questions, and often function as a conscience of the effort to implement inclusive school change.
4.  Social justice issues, including disability, must be incorporated throughout the curriculum.
5.  Creative use of time through implementation of innovative school schedules is essential.
6.  General and special education teachers with new job descriptions that reflect shared responsibility for all students must collaborate to design the curriculum, teach, and evaluate students.
7.  Tracking must be eliminated, and most classes should be grouped heterogeneously.
8.  The curriculum must be thematic, performance oriented, constructivist, and based on high achievement standards for every student.

From Fisher, D., Sax, C., & Jorgensen, C.M. (1998). Philosophical foundations of inclusive, restructuring schools. In C.M. Jorgensen, *Restructuring high schools for all students: Taking inclusion to the next level* (pp. 31–32). Baltimore: Paul H. Brookes Publishing Co.; reprinted by permission.

do not resist change, they resist being changed. The way we think about change, whether in the context of education (Fullan, 1993; Sergiovanni, 1994), organizations (Bergquist, 1993; Senge, 1990), or leadership (Heifetz, 1994; Kostner, 1994), is gradually shifting from a focus on identification and classification of details to a quest for understanding relationships among the parts. This more holistic— postmodern, if you will—way of thinking, or *systems thinking,* emerged in the late 19th and early 20th centuries. Evolving first as a concept in the fields of biology, psychology, ecology, and quantum theory (Capra, 1994), professionals began to frame their thinking around connectedness and relationships. To conceptualize change from a systems perspective requires that internal and external influences be considered and that the change process be understood as being complex; nonlinear; continuous; and difficult, if not impossible, to control. Fullan (1993) summarized eight basic lessons of what he described as the new paradigm of change that take into consideration similar tenets that others described:

Lesson 1: What matters cannot be mandated. (The more complex the change, the less it can be forced.)

Lesson 2: Change is a journey, not a blueprint. (Change is nonlinear, loaded with uncertainty and excitement, and sometimes perverse.)

Lesson 3: Problems are friends. (Problems are inevitable, and learning cannot take place without them.)

Lesson 4: Vision and strategic planning come later. (Avoid premature visions and planning.)

Lesson 5: Individualism and collectivism must have equal power. (There are no one-sided solutions to isolation and group thinking.)

Lesson 6: Neither centralization nor decentralization works. (Both top-down and bottom-up strategies are necessary.)

Lesson 7: Connection with the wider environment is critical for success. (The best organizations learn externally as well as internally.)

Lesson 8: Every person is a change agent. (Change is too important to leave to the experts; personal mind-set and mastery are the ultimate protection.)

Bringing resources, programs, and people together instead of categorizing and separating them is evident in many educational reforms. The work of Oakes (1985) blew an irrefutable hole in the logic of tracking students, although in many places the practice perseveres. Schools are placing less emphasis on categorizing and labeling students into homogeneous groups and are increasing recognition of the talents of individuals within heterogeneous groupings of students. Even the territorialism of high school academic departments is being challenged as schools restructure to facilitate interdisciplinary instruction. On a national level, federal education funding is more likely to support systemwide change efforts than individual demonstrations of recommended practices. Overall, more emphasis is being placed on critical thinking skills, collaboration strategies, and creative ways to apply and demonstrate knowledge. Educational leadership encouraging this shift is embracing and promoting the concept of a global community.

Systems thinking also helps leaders interact more effectively with schools, communities, or other social organizations. First, underlying every system is a fundamental purpose for its existence (Schalock, Fredericks, Dalke, & Alberto, 1994). Next, this purpose must be incorporated into a shared vision that is based on clear values (Heifetz, 1994). Senge explained this concept well: "Vision paints the picture of what we want to create. Systems thinking reveals how we have created what we currently have" (1990, p. 231).

## Approaches to Inclusive School Change

Just as change occurs at different paces, it is built on different priorities. Frameworks for school change have been designed to match the pace and priorities set internally by the school or district or externally by state initiatives or federal funding priorities. Factors such as the size of the district, community support, leadership and management styles, and available funding contribute not only to the success of reforms but also to the approaches that are used. The different approaches to change can be conceptualized in many ways. Some change occurs on a case-by-case basis; other change efforts are piloted. Some approaches can best be characterized by a planned phase-in, others as total conversions. Each of these four approaches provides insights and lessons to guide attempts at change. These approaches to change are described in this chapter in reference to inclusive education reform. Although overlap between the approaches occurs, each of these categories has specific characteristics that, taken together, can be viewed as a continuum. Figure 1 details the benefits and limitations of each approach (NASBE Study Group on Special Education, 1995). As actual schools and their change processes are considered, some of the distinctions outlined in the framework might blur. Nonetheless, it is important to consider the variety of ways in which schools have addressed the need for change.

***Case-by-Case Approach*** In schools across the United States, students with disabilities are educated alongside their peers without disabilities based on individual requests by parents; advocates; or, in some cases, special educators and related-services providers (e.g., speech-language therapists, psychologists). The key strength of this approach is that transition is smooth and gradual. Proponents of this approach report that, by including students with disabilities on a case-by-case basis, administrators, general education teachers, and

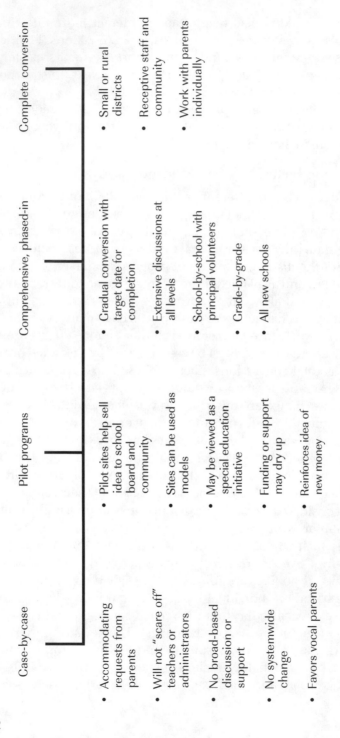

| Case-by-case | Pilot programs | Comprehensive, phased-in | Complete conversion |

- Accommodating requests from parents
- Will not "scare off" teachers or administrators
- No broad-based discussion or support
- No systemwide change
- Favors vocal parents

- Pilot sites help sell idea to school board and community
- Sites can be used as models
- May be viewed as a special education initiative
- Funding or support may dry up
- Reinforces idea of new money

- Gradual conversion with target date for completion
- Extensive discussions at all levels
- School-by-school with principal volunteers
- Grade-by-grade
- All new schools

- Small or rural districts
- Receptive staff and community
- Work with parents individually

Figure 1.  Inclusive school change implementation continuum. (*Source:* NASBE Study Group on Special Education, 1995.)

the school at large are not scared off by the change process of converting to inclusive classrooms.

The case-by-case approach, however, has several drawbacks. Those schools and districts that have used this approach are much less likely to have widely discussed inclusive education. They are also much less likely to have conducted comprehensive professional development programs for the teachers who will be supporting the students with disabilities. Furthermore, including students in this ad hoc fashion does not require the individual school or the school district to consider how the system must change to promote inclusion. At the same time, resources to support individual students and maintain fully operational separate systems are hard to coordinate. As a result, the cost of an inclusive support system may be unnecessarily inflated or exaggerated.

In addition, the case-by-case method favors families and students who have strong connections to the school and the community and who have the resources and the courage to communicate their needs to school officials. Those less likely to make such requests include the majority of parents, especially those parents who view school officials as authority figures who should not be crossed, are uninformed about other options, are simply unable to communicate their concerns about separate special education programs, or are focused on the day-to-day family issues. Last, the case-by-case approach too often is initiated only as an adversarial action (i.e., as a challenge to established school procedure). Under such conditions, acceptance, replication, and collaboration may be overshadowed by threats, intimidation, and a minimal amount of collaboration.

***Pilot Programs*** Next on the change effort continuum are districts that work on inclusion by initiating special pilot programs, usually funded through special project grants. The benefit of this approach, district officials explain, is that the pilot programs usually provide district administrators with evaluation data that can be used to sell inclusion to the school board and other stakeholders in the community. In addition, pilot sites can then serve as models for district personnel to visit as part of the education and communication stages of the planning process.

Drawbacks to initiating inclusion via specially funded pilot programs are inevitable. First, specially funded projects are typically initiated by the district special education director and are seen as a special education initiative. Thus, it may be difficult to expand the project into a systemwide initiative that would benefit all children. The pilot program, although endorsed, may not be integrated into the district's major priorities (e.g., its literacy program). Second, many districts suffer from "projectitis." That is, the district is accustomed to bringing in many special projects and grants for new initiatives, only to see them abandoned when the special funding runs out. This circumstance seems to be particularly true of large, inner-city districts. Superintendents who have initiated special pilot programs with the intent of gradually expanding into districtwide, systemic change have sometimes left the district before such expansion gets under way. Remember, the average tenure of a school superintendent is approximately 3 years. Those districts that have created inclusive schools entirely through special projects are vulnerable to the charge that inclusion can be successful only with an increase in funding. Few attempts are made in pilot projects to convert resources and build new capacities. Pilot programs too often characterize an add-on approach instead of a structural change.

*Phase-In Approach*  Many districts phase in inclusive education in a comprehensive but gradual manner. One of the strengths of this method is a clear understanding that, within a certain period of time, all students will be offered inclusive, age-appropriate classrooms in the school that they would attend if they did not have a disability. One of the drawbacks is a lack of consensus that such an understanding is clear. Others support or go along with the approach because it merely creates an alternative in unmet service delivery, but it is not a step in systematically changing that delivery.

Districts phase in inclusive education in a variety of ways. In some districts, the central administration asks for principal volunteers to be the district leaders in creating inclusive classrooms. These principals usually work with their staff to determine which teachers in their building would like to be the first to include students with disabilities in their classes. Volunteer teachers are offered joint planning time with special educators and other critical friends who may facilitate training, help with strategizing, and connect them to valuable resources. In some instances, innovative principals have worked to obtain additional funds to enhance the classroom program of participating teachers. With this positive reinforcement, other teachers usually follow suit and volunteer to participate in future years. Alternatively, some principal volunteers offer staff members who feel they are not ready to create inclusive classrooms an opportunity to transfer without penalty to another school. As principals make an increased commitment to change, they must make decisions about members of their staff who refuse to accept diverse learners in their classrooms. Eventually, those teachers may be asked to consider working elsewhere.

In many districts, inclusive education is phased in grade by grade, usually starting with kindergarten and adding the next one or two grades each year. Alternatively, some districts begin inclusive education for the entry grade in every school in the district. For example, the high schools in the district would begin providing inclusive education to ninth graders, and the middle schools would begin providing inclusive education to the sixth graders. In these cases, all students start school in classrooms of diverse learners and continue in inclusive environments as they progress through their school careers. Teachers and administrators report that, with this type of implementation, the general education students themselves become key elements in training teachers as they advance through the grades. Equally as important, students without disabilities help to increase the comfort level of the adults who have never interacted with students who have goals and expectations that are different from those of their peers. That is, the general education students often know about characteristics and behaviors of individual students with disabilities that they are able to share with teachers in subsequent years.

Some districts have combined one of the previously mentioned methods with a district policy that any new school opened in the system is opened as an inclusive school. Principals who have opened inclusive schools and hired teachers based on this philosophy have reported great success in building a cohesive staff and a school culture supportive of inclusion from the school's very inception. Parents often express concern, however, about phased-in approaches when they believe that their children are left out of the effort. Imagine a tenth grader at a school that develops a 4-year plan starting with ninth graders. That tenth-grade student may exit school before the effort is accomplished.

**Complete Conversions** Some districts have implemented inclusion on a districtwide basis, making the complete change in a period of 1 or 2 school years. These tend to be small or rural schools that are able to operate flexibly, have a small central administration and a receptive staff, and serve an accepting community. In these districts, the administration often has held extensive planning conferences with individual parents of students with disabilities because this approach equates with massive change of placement for the students in that district.

Regardless of which process districts have used to move from the drawing board to the classroom, several administrators have reported that inclusion has spread through their districts faster than they had anticipated. Teachers and principals want to create inclusive environments as other teachers and principals experiment with inclusion in their schools, as they see positive gains for all students in those schools, as teachers are reinvigorated in their work, and as the district supports and rewards the efforts of staff in inclusive schools.

## CONCLUSIONS

To be inclusive and effective, the stories and reflections of the following chapters focus on change efforts in secondary schools or those interested in reforming secondary school practices. Examples of reform efforts undertaken by high schools in both rural and urban communities are described. Each of the schools described in this book started at a different place, moved at a different pace, and chose its unique priorities carefully. Nonetheless, they all have become more inclusive as they have restructured the way in which they provide education for all students. Although no prescriptions are given for creating inclusive, restructuring schools, it is hoped that readers will see themselves and their schools somewhere in this book. Readers are encouraged to draw from each of the stories and apply appropriate components to their own situations. Remember, we all are still learning. . . .

# 3

# Personal and Professional Evolutions About Inclusive Education

David Zaino

In the late 1970s, my university preservice training program emphasized a functional skills curriculum and systematic instruction as the recommended practices for educating students with significant disabilities. Special education was at a crossroads of sorts. The developmental approach was giving way to a focus on functional skills. I embraced this precept as I began my first year of teaching in a homogeneous, self-contained classroom in a sheltered workshop for transition-age students. It seemed logical at the time that token economies, successive approximations, and systematic behavioral approaches would help students with significant disabilities acquire the necessary skills to become more productive and independent citizens. At the very least, it prepared my students to enter a segregated adult world in which they might be expected to work rather than continue to be viewed as "hopeless." Despite my satisfaction with teaching students labeled *severely handicapped* (SH), I was encouraged to leave the womb of the sheltered workshop transition program, and in 1983 I went to teach at a comprehensive high school campus.

On my new high school campus, Valley View, there were new challenges to face (e.g., general education students and teachers, six-bell schedules, administrative responsibilities). My curriculum and the organizational structure of the school, however, were similar to what I had experienced at the workshop. Valley View's regionalized program emphasized functional skills and community-based education, and all students with disabilities were homogeneously grouped into seven self-contained classrooms on campus. I and my colleagues determined some students to be diploma bound, and we focused on the completion of competency requirements within differentiated standards. Students who were not seeking a diploma received a certificate of attendance signifying the completion of their special education program. Both diploma- and non–diploma-seeking students were tracked in special education classes and attended a separate graduation ceremony. The students and teachers in the program in effect were a school within a school, in which the students took a separate journey. They had a different schedule, a different curriculum, and a different set of peers and teachers from other students in the school. Even though the program was community based, it never occurred to my colleagues and me that this separate journey might not be preparing all of Valley View's students to be cooperative members of the community.

Although I had been a member of the Valley View special education staff, I had not really functioned as or been accepted as a member of the Valley View faculty. I encountered many barriers, but perhaps the greatest obstacle I faced was the lack of ownership and support from the general education administration for myself or my students. At Valley View, a regionalized program, a special education administrator located on the campus coped with all special education problems.

Eleven years later, in 1994, I transferred to Mountain View High School as part of the district's decentralization effort in special education. Many of the students who had been in the regionalized program would attend their neighborhood school. Mountain View had never enrolled students with significant disabilities until my class arrived. I was forced to reexamine my experiences, biases, and practices concerning the placement and education of students with disabilities. I realized that the first step to including students was to include myself in the school community. Despite old traditions of administrative and structural division, I and my colleagues were able to tap into a special culture that existed at Mountain View. Once that culture was exposed, it turned out to be an essential ingredient for creating a genuine sense of acceptance and belonging, particularly for one student, Christina.

## Christina's Journey

Christina's journey illustrates the extremes of segregation and inclusion. For the first 14 years of her life, Christina had lived in a substandard orphanage in Romania for children labeled *ill-recoupable children*. Institutions were the primary domiciles for Romanians considered to be "unsalvageable" because of their physical or mental disabilities. In 1990, these deplorable conditions were brought into national prominence during a television broadcast, *Shame of a Nation: The Unsalvageable Children* (Barron, King, & Barron, 1984). Christina was featured in the broadcast. After a 2-year crusade and struggle to get these children out of Romania, John Upton, a resident of southern California, brought Christina and a number of other children with disabilities to the United States for adoption.

Christina, who is blind, began her secondary education at Mountain View High School in the fall of 1994 at the age of 13. Orphanage records indicated that Christina had few academic skills and could not read or complete basic tasks. Christina was placed in classes that emphasized community-based functional skills. She quickly learned to negotiate her way around the school and the community, and her level of vision was reassessed as legally blind (i.e., visual acuity of 20/200 [Snellen notation] in the better eye with best correction or a visual field that is no greater than 20°). She demonstrated skills and abilities beyond the expectations indicated by her records. Clearly, Christina legally qualified as having a significant disability. Nonetheless, she learned to initiate interactions with others, was eager to try new activities, and adapted to the school routine. During the next year and a half, Christina's individualized education program (IEP) goals addressed mobility, community education, and prevocational skills. She spent the majority of her school day off-campus with a group of other students with significant disabilities. Christina's adoptive family was physically active and interested in having Christina participate in sports. Her adoptive brothers and sisters were on the track team, and her new family expected her to try out for a sports team. Christina was the first student with significant disabilities to make the cross-country team.

Enrolling Christina in the physical education class seemed to be a logical next step to provide her with increased access to exercise equipment and practice with her peers. Christina's pioneering spirit and success gave me courage and experience to look again at my other students and their programs. One by one, I tried placing my students in general education classes according to their interests and skills. My experience led me to believe that this direction was appropriate. It represented a major shift in my program, however. I had a new context that included a new set of demands and relationships on which to build an even more functional program than the one originally designed. Knowing that teachers in other district schools were pursuing more inclusive experiences for their students, I decided to accept the challenge. I was ready to design and fully support typical high school schedules, in academic as well as nonacademic classes, for my 14- to 18-year-old students. I talked with my colleagues, and together in the fall of 1995 we approached faculty at San Diego State University with a request for support.

In partnership with faculty members at San Diego State, my school initiated efforts to include students with disabilities fully in the general education program. Contrary to popular logic, my program began with five students who had significant disabilities. Christina became a critical member of the inclusion team for the other four students as a trailblazer for the whole idea of inclusive education. She had already developed an impressive social network with her peers on the track and cross-country teams and in other extracurricular activities. Natural supports from her peers became a valuable resource as we added more general education classes to her schedule and solicited the involvement of other high school students and faculty members. Her wit, charm, and tenaciousness helped to entrench inclusive attitudes among others at the school toward students with significant disabilities, attitudes that were unprecedented at the high school. Christina unintentionally became the program's ambassador. The survival instincts that Christina had developed in the Romanian orphanage, in addition to her desire to achieve and experience everything that life has to offer, taught me and my colleagues all about expectations and resilience.

As a senior Christina attended academic and elective classes throughout the six-period day. She enrolled in the publications class, in which she worked on the school yearbook. During her 4 years at Mountain View High School, she participated in athletic endeavors, including the cross-country, track and field, water polo, and swim teams. Was Christina's success a result of inclusive education or an inherent desire to be included? I believe they were mutually reinforcing. Despite Christina's contributions to the program's efforts, students with and without disabilities had such a limited history of past exposure to, interaction with, and school experiences in common with each other that their lack of familiarity continued to be an obstacle to increased social connections and academic supports. As I reflected on these experiences, successes, and shortcomings, I decided to enter a graduate program.

## EVOLUTION OF INCLUSIVE EDUCATION

My journey from the sheltered workshop to a segregated community-based program to including my students as supported and participating members of their high school provoked my intellectual curiosity. I chose to investigate the movement toward inclusive education as a major educational reform. I then learned to see inclusive education as part of a larger reform agenda. A number of factors have provided the impetus for supporting these inclusive reforms and have led to a response to continued reports of limited outcomes for special education students. These factors include equity and rights issues, parental advocacy and litigation, and the high costs of separate special education (Lipsky & Gartner, 1997). At the same time, many of the reform and restructuring efforts occurring in general education have embraced practices long supported in special education (Jorgensen, 1998). Some school districts have initiated broad school restructuring efforts that include special education and general education students; most, however, have not (Lipsky & Gartner, 1997). Perhaps if there were more recognition of the common goals and practices for all students, the need for separate educational journeys might decrease (National Association of State Boards of Education [NASBE] Study Group on Special Education, 1995).

Negative attitudes and perceptions toward people with disabilities continue to define and limit expectations for children with disabilities and to influence special education practices and placement patterns (Fisher, 1996; Lipsky & Gartner, 1997). Without changes in attitude among teachers and administrators, fundamental practices and assumptions will limit the impact of inclusive education. As educators concerned with other marginalized people have argued, a shift away from a deficit orientation to an ability orientation must occur (Nieto, 1996). The need that students with disabilities may have for additional support and accommodation must be viewed as a means of supporting their abilities rather than be viewed as masking their deficits.

The special education bureaucracy itself may limit the vision and expectations of individuals with disabilities and, in turn, perpetuate restrictive attitudes. Consider the biased perceptions displayed in the 1992 federal definition of *mental retardation*:

*Mild retardation:* Children capable of becoming self-sufficient and learning academic skills through the upper elementary grades.

*Moderate retardation:* Children who are not able to profit from regular instruction or from instruction for the mildly handicapped.

*Severe retardation:* Children who are significantly subaverage in intellectual functioning and who have concurrent deficits or impairments in adaptive functioning. This is a developmental disorder whose onset occurs before the age of 18. (cited in Lipsky & Gartner, 1997, p. 8)

Legal and professional definitions and descriptions of students with significant disabilities have been described in a variety of ways that conveyed hopelessness and despair, using terms such as "extremely debilitating, inflexibly incapacitated, or uncompromisingly crippled" (McDonnell, Hardman, McDonnell, & Kiefer-O'Donnell, 1995, p. 3). Others have defined *disability* as a discrepancy from what is typical. Justen proposed such a definition:

> The "severely handicapped" refers to those individuals age 21 and younger who are functioning at a general developmental level of half or less than the level which would be expected on the basis of chronological age and who manifest learning and/or behavioral problems of such magnitude and significance that they require extensive structure in learning situations if their education needs are to be well served. (1976, p. 5)

Consider the not-so-subtle differences between these former descriptions and a more contemporary one posed by Meyer, Peck, and Brown:

> [People with disabilities] include individuals of all ages who require extensive ongoing support in more than one major life activity in order to participate in integrated community settings and to enjoy a quality of life that is available to citizens with fewer or more disabilities. Support may be required for life activities such as mobility, communication, self-care, and learning as necessary for independent living, employment, and self-sufficiency. (1991, p. 19)

The focus of the previous definition is on supports, not on deficits. The responsibility for identifying and providing those supports becomes a challenge to the education service system, and typical performance and lifestyles presume access to such supports.

Prior to the passage of the Education for All Handicapped Children Act of 1975 (PL 94-142), the majority of students with significant disabilities did not attend public schools. One major feature of PL 94-142 is its least restrictive environment (LRE) provision and the related bias to ensure implementation of the most inclusive placement feasible. U.S. Department of Education (1995) data indicated that, as of the early 1990s, educators had failed to implement the LRE provision consistently. Clearly, large numbers of students with disabilities had not been educated with their peers without disabilities. Lipsky and Gartner (1997) pointed out, furthermore, the extraordinary range of placement patterns in their examination of 1) placing students with disabilities in classes with their chronological age peers versus placing them in classes with their mental age peers, 2) disability, and 3) state practices. Other researchers have suggested that even when inclusive practices are more prevalent, such placements are difficult to report because accounting systems presume that such students would not be included or that schools are financially paralyzed for pursuing such practices (Roach, Halvorsen, Zeph, Giugno, & Caruso, 1997). The failure to provide placements consistent with the bias of the law and the difficulty in reporting them both suggest administrative policies and practices that presume that such placements are unexpected. Do the negative perceptions and definitions of the past still linger in the minds and the pens of special and general education policy makers? Perhaps only a new generation who will grow up with experiences that reinforce a new set of perceptions and values can close the history books of deficit-centered thinking.

Curriculum innovations have evolved since the 1970s. Innovations have affected programs, practices, and educational placements. During this time, policy and practice have operated within the concept of a continuum of placements model, identified in PL 94-142 as the LRE provisions. The continuum of placements was designed to provide a full range of services for individuals with disabilities from the most restrictive to the least restrictive environments. From the inception of the continuum of placements model, common practice and common logic have been to place individuals with disabilities who require more intensive services in the most restrictive environments. The model is challenged by many as a means of perpetuating unnecessary segregation. Furthermore, some of the most pioneering work in inclusive education has been done with students manifesting the most severe disabilities. Specifically, Hitzing (1980) identified six pitfalls of the continuum model:

1.  Students with severe disabilities get stuck at the wrong, or the most restrictive, end of the continuum.
2.  The most restrictive placements do not prepare students for the least restrictive placements.
3.  There are always bottlenecks in the continuum.
4.  The continuum implies that students must move to receive services, especially if they develop new skills.
5.  Resources, especially financial resources, are concentrated at the most restrictive end of the continuum.
6.  The continuum emphasizes placements, not services.

The original intent of the Education for All Handicapped Children Act was to ensure that all children with disabilities receive a free appropriate public education. Despite the mandate that students with disabilities be educated in the LRE, concerns focused on access and process rather than on the outcomes of instruction. Sufficient data are available, however, to conclude that outcomes for students with disabilities who participate in a separate special education system are extremely limited (Wagner, 1993). Low student graduation rates, high unemployment and arrest rates, limited residential independence, and limited access to postsecondary education and training are the outcomes of students with disabilities under the current service delivery of noninclusive education. Given the limited academic and social gains of students in special education, it is logical to consider student placement as a contributor to poor student outcomes. In addition, the very existence of the LRE provisions, built on a line or continuum of placements, warrants more critical review than policy makers, researchers, practitioners, and advocates seem to be willing to provide.

Since PL 94-142 took effect, a separate and parallel bureaucracy has been created to serve students with disabilities. I saw it at Valley View, and it lingers just outside the doors of Mountain View. The outcomes for students with disabilities are undergoing close scrutiny, however, and questions are being raised about the quality and efficacy of the special education system (NASBE, 1992). The widespread failures that are documented in the special education system provide a strong basis for change. Many parents and professionals have come to believe that implementing an inclusive philosophy of education in schools would be a better approach not only for students with disabilities but also for their peers without disabilities.

## BENEFITS OF INCLUSIVE EDUCATION

Inclusion is predicated on the assumption of starting with what is considered typical and then making adaptations as needed for other students rather than focusing on trying to fix students with disabilities to make them fit into an inflexible "norm." Inclusion is not a place or a method of delivering instruction; it is a philosophy of supporting all children in their learning with a byproduct of strengthening the entire system. Inclusive practices are a part of the very culture of a school or a school district and define how students, teachers, administrators, and others view the potential of children and their place in their school and their community. The inclusive philosophy of supported education embraces a fundamental belief that all children can learn and achieve. I and my colleagues have worked hard to develop high school schedules for my students that reflect the same vigor, flexibility, and variation provided to other students. We also work hard to articulate purpose, functionality, individuality, and support. The question remains, however, Do students benefit from inclusive education? For me, the answer to this question is clear. My professional practice and my commitment to inclusive education reform are affirmed by the benefits that I see my students have gained. I next summarize these benefits in four areas: adult outcomes, academic benefits, social benefits, and language acquisition.

## Adult Outcomes

Success for high school students is often measured in outcomes such as meaningful work, a place to live, and personal fulfillment that includes a social network of friends and family. These outcomes are equally valid for students with disabilities. Unfortunately, longitudinal research on post–high school outcomes has supported the assumption that a significant disparity exists between those outcomes that students with and without disabilities have achieved (Wagner, 1993). Is it not reasonable to assume that to prepare students with disabilities to live in inclusive communities as adults, they should grow up in an inclusive environment in which they interact with their peers? Positive postschool adjustment is one benefit of inclusion (NASBE, 1992). The relationships developed in school with peers without disabilities could provide the supports necessary to establish the connections and skills necessary to make a successful transition into adulthood (Fisher, Sax, Pumpian, Rodifer, & Kreikemeirer, 1997).

The National Longitudinal Transition Study (NLTS) (Wagner & Blackorby, 1996) examined the relationship between time spent by students with disabilities in high school general education classes and the postschool outcomes for those students between 1985 and 1990. Researchers involved with the NLTS found a direct correlation between the amount of time students spent in general education classes and their successful adult outcomes (U.S. Department of Education, 1995). The relationship between increased time in general education classes and improved student competencies and better employment, residential independence, postsecondary education, and increased graduation options warrants much more serious attention from policy makers.

## Academic Benefits

Surprisingly few studies investigating the effect of membership in inclusive classrooms on the academic achievement of students with and without disabilities have been conducted (Hunt & Goetz, 1997). Hunt, Staub, Alwell, and Goetz (1994) investigated achievement of all students in cooperative learning groups at one elementary school. Students in their study were not negatively affected in terms of the academic objectives identified for the math unit. The results of the Hunt and colleagues study contributed to the emerging literature suggesting that high and average achievers gain from cooperative learning just as do students who are not achieving as well as their peers (Stevens & Slavin, 1995).

Sharpe, York, and Knight (1994) conducted a pretest–posttest study to analyze the academic performance of general education students who attended an elementary school in a rural, east central Minnesota school district. Academic performance was measured by grades on report cards in the areas of reading, mathematics, and spelling as well as by conduct and effort. The results indicated that no significant differences were observed in students' academic or behavioral performance between classes that included a child with significant disabilities and classes that did not. Other authors have reported positive parental perceptions especially when comparing academic outcomes before and after implementation of inclusion (Gibb et al., 1997; Ryndak, Downing, Jacqueline, & Morrison, 1995). Ryndak and colleagues (1995) reported that parents of children with disabilities attributed their children's increased acquisition of academic skills to their participation in general education classes.

## Social Benefits

The positive effects of students' social interactions, specifically with regard to social acceptance and membership, are well documented (Evans, Salisbury, Palombaro, Berryman, & Hollowood, 1992; Schorr, 1997). Studies of sustained classroom engagement (Hollowood,

Salisbury, Rainforth, & Palombaro, 1994; Hunt et al., 1994), increased social networks (Fryxell & Kennedy, 1995; Kennedy & Itkonen, 1994), facilitated peer interaction (Hanline, 1993; Janney & Snell, 1996), and the development of friendships (Staub, Schwartz, Gallucci, & Peck, 1994) lend further support for the importance of social acceptance and membership. One of the greatest barriers to the development of friendships between individuals with and without disabilities has been their lack of opportunity for social interaction (Falvey, 1995). According to Lutfiyya (1988), proximity and frequency are prerequisites essential for the development of friendships.

Since the early 1980s, social contact has been viewed as a critical determinant in the movement toward inclusive education by parents and professionals. Social contact plays an important role in the development of children's attitudes toward their peers with disabilities (Meyer, Park, Grenot-Scheyer, Schwartz, & Harry, 1998). Attitudes developed at a young age are often carried well into adulthood (Turnbull & Broniki, 1986). The connections to the school and the community that children with disabilities develop while in school can serve as a guide and support for maintaining such connections as adults (Falvey, 1995).

## Language Acquisition

Communication is a fundamental component of the quality of life and interaction among people. It is an essential ingredient in the development of friendships and meaningful interactions between students with and without disabilities. Inclusive classrooms provide opportunities for students' developing new relationships and engaging in social and cooperative activities. Such classrooms also provide for a rich learning environment full of language (Downing, Eichinger, & Williams, 1997). It is logical to conclude that segregated environments, unlike inclusive ones, diminish opportunities for the quality and scope of language development (Calculator & Jorgensen, 1994). Limited opportunities for socialization and communication for students with significant disabilities are untenable.

Significant improvement in the area of communication skills for students with disabilities who experience full-time placement in inclusive classrooms has been documented. One case study focused on a student with significant disabilities who participated in general education classes at an inclusive high school (Bagg-Rizzo, 1996). This study provided an in-depth look at the changes that were prompted by a shift in placement from a segregated to an inclusive classroom environment. Through multiple sources including records, interviews, and observations, the results demonstrated marked improvement in academic areas as well as in socialization and communication skills. Bagg-Rizzo, in Chapter 4, concludes that the communication skills of Michelle, a student with disabilities, improved significantly because of her participation in general education classes.

General educators have also identified improved communication as one of many beneficial outcomes in their classrooms. Giangreco, Dennis, Cloninger, Edelman, and Schattman (1993) examined attitudes and perceptions of general education teachers whose classes included a student with a significant disability.

Parents' perceptions of their children's educational outcomes are also crucial. Ryndak and colleagues (1995) investigated the perspectives of 13 parents whose children with significant disabilities were full-time members of general education classrooms. The parents were questioned about the degree to which their children's inclusive program had successfully met the children's educational and social needs. Interview questions focused on skill acquisition before and after inclusion, perceived benefits of inclusive education, and their vision of their children's future as a result of inclusive educational placement. All of the parents reported a dramatic growth in the speech, language, and communication skills of their children following placement in inclusive environments. Specifically, respondents described more receptive and expressive language, increased fluency and clarity, greater conversational initiative, and an increase in vocabulary.

Students without disabilities have also achieved progress in the acquisition of communication when students with significant disabilities participate with them in inclusive classroom environments. Fisher, Sax, and Jorgensen recounted a high school student's view of how the communication skills of one of her peers with disabilities increased:

> In one of my classes, I met Jesse, who uses a wheelchair and is unable to communicate with words. I knew she was learning because she began to smile and raise her head when you said something or did something that she liked. If Jesse had been confined to one room, she would not have been exposed to many different people and would not have raised her head. That was her way of responding. (1998, p. 30)

In addition to positive outcomes from anecdotal reports, Hunt and colleagues (1994) demonstrated that three elementary school-age students who experienced multiple severe disabilities could acquire basic communication skills and motor skills within the context of cooperative learning groups in the general education classroom. With gradually fading assistance from project staff, the members of the group without disabilities were able to provide prompts and cues to promote acquisition of the targeted communication and motor skills. The results demonstrated that all three students with disabilities generalized those skills during follow-up sessions to activities with other members of a newly formed group. These results suggest that, at least within the structure of cooperative learning groups, adequate opportunity, potential support, and motivation are available for the students with multiple severe disabilities to acquire basic communication and motor objectives.

Erickson, Koppenhaver, Yoder, and Nance (1997) examined how the general classroom influenced literacy learning and the role of assistive technology in school-based literacy activities. The researchers employed a qualitative case study to evaluate authentically a student's progress from a special school serving only students with significant disabilities to full inclusive classroom environments. The results indicated that the student, Jordan, gradually increased his communication through the development of literacy skills and the assistance of an augmentative and alternative communication device within the context of inclusive classrooms. Using a Dynavox, which is a voice-output communication device, Jordan was able to develop literacy skills in generating his own messages to become a more active participant in the class. Jordan increased his communicative competence and his ability to create his own messages independently. He also developed motor and visual skills beyond his professionally assessed ability. Jordan's progress was facilitated with an appropriate mode of communication and an inclusive environment that increased his opportunity and desire to communicate.

It is reasonable to create authentic rather than artificial conditions that promote the development of interaction and communication skills. Students with disabilities should be afforded opportunities to develop their communication and social skills alongside their peers without disabilities (Calculator & Jorgensen, 1994). Inclusive school environments offer unlimited possibilities for both.

## CONCLUSIONS

The movement toward inclusive education has forced me to examine the issues surrounding the education of students with disabilities in general education classrooms. Benefits and outcomes require that policies, practices, and historical presumptions be reexamined. Although the debate among educators and policy makers regarding the ethics and efficacy of inclusive education continues, the research evidence is compelling. I have no doubt that the inclusion of students with disabilities in the general education program provides new opportunities for the next generation and many challenges for the educators of this generation. Mere placement changes are insufficient without continued attention to educational reform (i.e., changes in teaching and learning). If the competence and involvement of students with severe disabilities in the general education program are met with creativity in providing supports that demonstrate their capabilities, the benefits of and preparation for life realized in inclusive schools should exceed expectations. If inclusive education continues to be viewed as an experiment, if people with disabilities continue to be perceived only in terms of their deficits, and if people continue to assume that segregation is the model and inclusion is the radical exception, then new opportunities will be lost and the skeptics will be proved correct. My teaching and research contributions are a result of my experiences learning from Christina and many other students. The adult outcomes that I have come to expect and that my students realize are far beyond what was expected or achieved in the sheltered world of the past.

4

# Portraits of Inclusion

Eileen Bagg-Rizzo

When I became a high school English teacher, I never expected to have students with disabilities in my classes. My teacher education program in Oklahoma provided me with a wealth of knowledge about American literature, literary theory and criticism, genres of writing, and instruction strategies. No one ever suggested—nor did I ever imagine—that these strategies were applicable to students with disabilities. As an undergraduate student in the English department, I also had the somewhat naive perspective that my future students would be a small, homogeneous group, all of whom shared my passion for literature. I never imagined being asked to share my passion with the whole student body. I did not even realize how diverse and heterogeneous that student body would be. Thinking back even further, as a high school student in New Mexico, I assumed that my tenth-grade English class looked like the class that I would eventually teach. Students with disabilities were not members of my class then; I had no reason to believe that the classes I would eventually teach would be any different.

I cannot imagine excluding any student, however. My classes are a lively mix of students from different backgrounds, with varying levels of passion and understanding. In an effort to meet the needs of my students better, I returned to school to earn certificates in advanced placement instruction and English as a second language. Despite my success with teaching tracked English courses, my cognitive dissonance increased. I believed that all students could learn and that everyone belonged, yet I felt that my practices were inconsistent with these beliefs. I challenged myself and then my colleagues to detrack our courses.

An important step toward detracking classes in our high school was the placement of students with disabilities in general education academic courses. One of the first students enrolled in my tenth-grade English class was Michelle. Although I was convinced that it was the right thing to do, I was not sure how to proceed or whether I could really succeed at teaching her in my class. I decided to pursue my master's degree with a focus on inclusive educational reform. Having just completed a graduate course in action research, I decided to focus my master's project on the outcomes of inclusive practices. Michelle and her family provided me an opportunity to consider inclusion from an insider's perspective. In this chapter, I share the portrait of inclusion that Michelle and I created.

## FRAMING THE PORTRAITS OF INCLUSION

I use a case study to describe Michelle's experiences as she moved from a self-contained special education environment to a general education high school classroom. Just as others who have used the case study method to describe change (e.g., Salisbury, Palombaro, & Hollowood, 1993), I focus specifically on changes in Michelle's academic achievement and social life at Kennedy High School (see also Chapter 5).

The most useful data collection tools were observations, record reviews, and interviews. I conducted classroom observations at random times for 10-minute intervals in a variety of content areas. I took notes on interactions between Michelle and her peers by writing down the observations in a running log format. I interviewed Michelle; her mother; and, over a period of 2 years, Michelle's peer tutors, her friends in the classes she attended, and her teachers. My questions were open ended and designed to focus on Michelle's social and academic achievements. In addition, I reviewed Michelle's cumulative file, which included individualized education programs (IEPs), observation logs, evaluations, assessments, and a student profile. Information from the classroom observations, interviews, and record reviews were analyzed for recurring themes. I was interested in the difference between Michelle's previous experiences in a self-contained classroom and her experiences in an inclusive high school environment.

## Portrait of Michelle

Michelle, the only survivor of triplets born prematurely, has cerebral palsy with partial paralysis on one side. She wears eyeglasses and requires large-print texts and additional visual cues. Michelle is verbal; however, she was described in her school records as having significant articulation problems, limited speech volume, and a slow speech pattern. Her special education file labels her as "severely handicapped."

Michelle's interests include listening to music, watching performances, learning about animals, talking on the telephone, being read to, and spending time with young children. She is responsible for completing chores at home such as cleaning her room, feeding the animals, and helping with the groceries. In her free time, she likes to visit her friends. Michelle's mother has described Michelle as "happy, cooperative, likes to meet new people but can be shy" (personal communication, November 1995). Michelle's writing skills are limited because of her lack of muscular control. Hand-over-hand support is necessary for her to type, and she needs a light touch on the hand when writing with a pencil or a pen.

Prior to attending Kennedy High School, Michelle attended self-contained special day classes (SDCs) at her junior high school. According to her student record, her junior high school class schedule was as follows:

| Time | Placement | Subject |
| --- | --- | --- |
| Period 1 | Special day class | Campus job |
| Period 2 | Special day class | Community/cooking |
| Period 3 | Special day class | Community/class work |
| Periods 4, 5 | Special day class | Adaptive physical education |
| Period 6 | Special day class | Grooming |
| Period 7 | Special day class | Recreation/leisure |

Michelle's junior high school IEP included goals and objectives to increase her use of functional reading, increase community skills, increase vocational independence, improve computer-operating skills, participate in adaptive physical education (APE), increase recreation and leisure skills, increase use of personal information, and increase verbal expression. The activities in the SDC that were designed to help Michelle achieve her goals included can crushing, setting the table, sorting silverware, table washing, swimming, working on a computer, and APE. In one observation, her teacher noted, "She can say her first and last name, her telephone number, the days of the week, and the school's name." It was also noted that she could recognize the following sight-words: rest room, men, women, entrance, exit, enter, out, down, push, pull, and walk. Michelle's teacher showed her pictures with the symbols of the sight-words, and she asked Michelle to say the appropriate word.

Data from Michelle's computer skills training showed progress in her ability to operate the computer. Her teacher noted that Michelle "could watch other people interact with a prepared program; she could use game buttons, paddles, and switches appropriately; she could insert and remove a disk properly; and she was able to turn the computer on and off." No information was provided regarding her typing ability.

Michelle also spent a designated part of the day on language development. Her teacher observed, "[Michelle] seems to be more comfortable talking in a small group of one or two people." In another written observation, a teacher noted that Michelle "failed to communicate with her peers in class." At the time of the observation, however, the teacher also recorded that "Michelle was seated next to a nonverbal student." Her teacher noted that Michelle told jokes and could talk in complete sentences. She also asked appropriate questions. She understood "who" and "where" questions, followed directions, and demonstrated a basic understanding of the English language.

Even though Michelle's official class schedule did not so indicate, Michelle did interact with some students without disabilities. Michelle's integration in the junior high consisted of her participation in a nonacademic, non–special education environment for 45 minutes per day. In addition to this elective rotation, Michelle attended all assemblies, joined in age-appropriate activities on and off campus with peers, and participated in a daily jogging program with her peers without disabilities. Michelle's mother expressed a strong desire to have her daughter spend more time with students without disabilities. She discussed in an interview that "Michelle doesn't like support services and prefers to go to a play group with friends without disabilities. If she is forced to go to support services, she cries and wants to go home."

When Michelle made the transition to Kennedy High School, her class schedule changed considerably. Kennedy used a block/quarter system in which students attend three 95-minute classes per day (Canady & Rettig, 1995). Each course lasts for 9 weeks. The second quarter of Michelle's tenth-grade schedule was as follows:

| Time | Placement | Subject |
|---|---|---|
| Block 1 | General education class | Tenth-grade English |
| Block 2 | General education class | Career and Family Studies |
| Block 3 | General education class | Chemistry |

The goals and objectives established in her high school IEP included the following: completing adapted classwork with assistance from peers and teachers with 75% accuracy, responding to scheduled class changes independently, improving keyboarding and computer skills, and improving compliant behavior by responding to reasonable requests the first time.

Compared with her junior high school experience, Michelle participated in different activities to meet her new goals, such as those she completed in her tenth-grade English class. The class was asked to write an essay in response to a Langston Hughes poem called "Dream Deferred." The objective of the essay was to describe the theme of the poem with regard to one of the following topics: prejudice, justice, or racism. The students worked in pairs to discuss the poem and then wrote essays that explained how the poem illustrated the topics. Michelle and her partner identified the themes of prejudice and racism in the poem. The essay was adapted to fit Michelle's ability by changing the format from the written essay to a pictorial essay. She and her partner looked through magazines for pictures that illustrated the points that the poem brought to light. When Michelle saw a picture she thought was appropriate, her partner helped her cut it out. Michelle glued the pictures onto the construction paper to create her essay. I submitted several completed essays to the school's newspaper for publication consideration. Michelle's report was one of those published. In Michelle's IEP review worksheet for tenth grade, her special education teacher noted, "[Michelle] enjoys illustrating key points with posters made from magazine pictures, she likes to use the computer to complete assignments, and she loves class presentations."

In chemistry, Michelle's class was assigned to write and present a paper on a vitamin or a mineral. Michelle chose vitamin A. The assignment was adapted to fit her needs by combining the written requirement with the oral presentation. She was asked to find six facts about vitamin A, so she used six large pieces of construction paper to illustrate the facts. On the front, she used pictures from magazines to provide her with a visual prompt of information she presented. For example, she stated, "Mothers who are nursing their babies need a lot of vitamin A." She cut out several pictures of mothers and babies and glued them to the front of the construction paper. On the back, she had a list of facts about mothers who are nursing and the importance of their getting enough vitamin A in their diets. She typed the list on the computer, enlarging the print for readability during her oral report. Michelle was nervous when she presented her report to the class, but she spoke loudly enough for everyone to hear.

Michelle's special education teacher made the following comments after reviewing Michelle's progress: "She has become more verbal in class, her tone of voice has improved, she has become comfortable walking around campus, and she interacts with her peers in class on a social and academic basis." Her teacher also described an experience in which Michelle went to a musical performance in the school's library. At the conclusion of the performance, Michelle independently went up to the stage and thanked the performer.

When asked about the consequences of Michelle's placement in general education classes, one teacher commented, "On the positive side, she has more opportunities to socialize with her peers without disabilities, she has access to the curriculum used in general education classes, she has improved her communication skills, and she has access to participate in all aspects of the high school experience." The teacher also noted, however, that "Michelle may need more time to adjust to the schedule changes in her day (from class to class), and support must be in place for her to benefit from class content." In a separate interview, Michelle's mother commented, "I am proud of my daughter and what she is doing. I want to keep her work age appropriate, and I want her to focus on her academics."

## COMPARING THE PORTRAITS
## OF SEPARATE AND INCLUSIVE EDUCATION

In comparing Michelle's IEP goals from her self-contained classroom placement with the goals in her inclusive education classroom, some similarities and many differences become apparent. At first glance, the goals of both placements seem similar. In both environments, Michelle received instruction in reading, computer skills, language development, and personal behavior. Upon a second look, however, the differences in the activities designed to meet her goals are obvious.

The activities in the self-contained class provided Michelle with multiple opportunities for practice, albeit in isolation. To meet her goal of improving functional vocabulary, for example, she looked at pictures of symbols and stated their meanings. In contrast, in her high school English class, Michelle developed her vocabulary and reading skills in context as she worked with a partner on a pictorial essay about the poem "Dream Deferred." Michelle discussed the poem with her classmates to identify salient themes and shared her ideas about pictures that illustrated the themes. In this activity, Michelle acquired new vocabulary and used that vocabulary in context. Similarly, her junior high school IEP goal for increasing computer skills resulted in Michelle's learning isolated skills. Her junior high school goal was considered to be successfully completed when she demonstrated that she could turn the computer on and off; when she could use buttons, paddles, or switches; and when she could watch others use prepared programs. In her high school general education classes, Michelle used the computer for many of her class projects. She acquired, improved, and generalized her typing skills by applying them in a variety of environments.

In the area of language development, Michelle's junior high self-contained classroom teacher reported that Michelle preferred to speak in small groups. At that time, Michelle had only nine other classmates, most of whom were not able to communicate verbally. Her teacher also noted that Michelle had difficulty with initiating interactions with her peers. Perhaps this was due to her limited access to students without disabilities. At Kennedy High School, I often observed Michelle enjoying interactions with her peers. The typical general education class size was approximately 33 students. She had many potential communication partners with whom to initiate and respond to interactions and conversations. In contrast with the difficulty Michelle had with language development in her junior high school class, Michelle enjoyed class presentations in high school. Michelle received a lot of positive attention from her peers when she completed her oral presentations.

Michelle met her junior high school IEP goals for using personal information by saying her first and last name with one-to-one assistance. In high school, Michelle independently wrote her name on all of her papers, had informal conversations about herself with her peers, and interacted with at least four teachers each day.

Differences in Michelle's opportunities to socialize were also evident when comparing her two education environments. When she participated in the self-contained special education class, she had contact with only her special education teacher, an adult aide, and nine other students with significant disabilities. For 45 minutes per day, she jogged with general education peers. Her opportunities for socializing with her peers were limited. I observed the same circumstances that my colleague, David Zaino, saw in a different high school (see Chapter 3). In Michelle's high school classes, she had countless opportunities to socialize—in fact, Michelle and her peers often socialized too much! Understanding the importance of socializing for all of my students, I developed more cooperative group activities in which students could talk about literature. Michelle had approximately 100 role models per day for learning how adolescents negotiate social relationships.

## CONCLUSIONS

Michelle and I both changed in many ways during her high school years. Michelle changed from a shy, quiet adolescent into an independent young lady. Her self-confidence increased, as did her circle of friends. She learned her class schedule, her way around the school, how to interact in small groups, and that learning could be fun. Michelle gained access to the core curriculum—a curriculum based on high standards for all students. Michelle explored parts of the high school culture that were previously inaccessible. She came to understand American societal issues as she studied and interacted with her peers.

I changed more than I expected. I learned that, given the right supports, all students can succeed in challenging academic courses. In addition, I learned that I was able to share my passion for literature with my students more effectively by changing some of my instruction strategies. Michelle was instrumental in teaching me that people demonstrate their understanding and knowledge in unique and often surprising ways. I know that I am only beginning to tap the talent and potential in my classroom.

Young people such as Christina and Michelle are labeled as students, but they have also been teachers. Dave Zaino and I are considered teachers, but we have been students as well. Christina helped Dave take his journey as a special educator and Michelle has enriched my sojourn as a faculty member of my high school's English department. I have been fortunate to teach in a school that encourages me to align my practices with my beliefs. In partnership with special educators, my colleagues and I have reorganized our supports and services for students with disabilities. In doing so, we have made a positive impact on the lives of thousands of students and adults. The tenth graders enrolled in my English classes still have much to learn; however, I am confident that their experiences with inclusive education have prepared them well for the future.

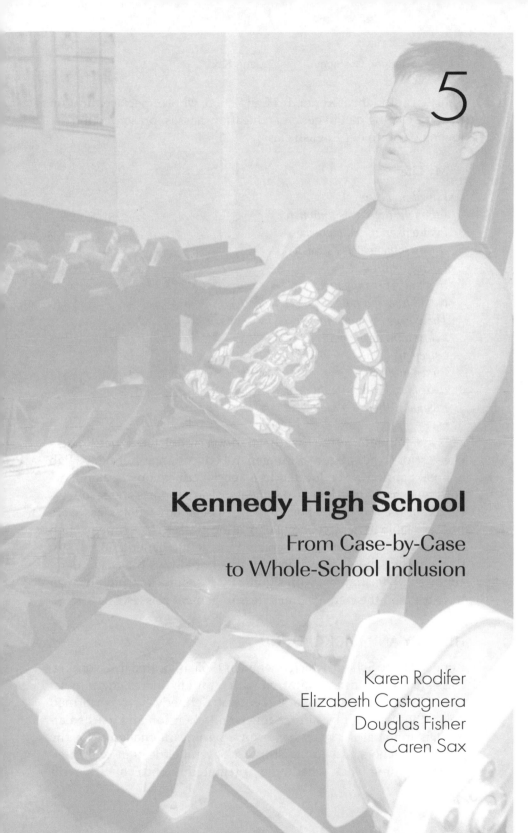

# 5

# Kennedy High School

## From Case-by-Case to Whole-School Inclusion

Karen Rodifer
Elizabeth Castagnera
Douglas Fisher
Caren Sax

Sabrina, a student at Kennedy High School whose special education needs are being met in general education classes, presented the following poem to her English class.

### My Life

*I lived in a dumpster.*
*I thought there was a monster.*
*I got woken up by a crash.*
*It was someone else's trash.*
*I played with dirt.*
*It got all over my shirt.*
*Now I live in a house.*
*There isn't even one mouse.*
*I can swim in the pool.*
*I sleep all night.*
*I have no fright.*
*Instead of living in a dumpster,*
*I would rather be a kid called a foster.*

This assignment was the first that Sabrina completed in her English class. Prior to her placement in general education at Kennedy High School, Sabrina was educated in a special education class and, according to her, "did a lot of worksheets." The supports and resources that Sabrina was once allocated in a special education class were now available to her in general education classes. At Kennedy High School, these resources have created incidental benefits for all students at the school. This, however, was not always the case. As recently as 1990, students with significant disabilities would not even have been on the campus, much less in general classes.

## HISTORY AND BACKGROUND

Kennedy High School, which opened in 1965, is located in a working-class area of southern California with a rapidly increasing population. Historically, the 1,850 students at Kennedy have performed below the state averages in reading comprehension and mathematics. Discipline at Kennedy has been a significant challenge for the school's teachers and administrators. Several education reform efforts, including block scheduling, integrated science courses, writing across the curriculum, and content area reading strategies, have been implemented. As one English teacher put it,

> Kennedy is a completely new school. The buildings may look old, but what happens in the classroom is totally cutting edge. We help students make connections across subject matter. We aren't traditional teachers; we are more like "conductors of learning." It is exciting to be part of students' senior projects and watch them create portfolios based on our performance standards that relate to their career objectives.

All students at Kennedy are expected to meet high standards in terms of both content and performance. Teachers, parents, and community members have established 15 expectations for students. These expectations, or performance standards, guide the curriculum and instruction for all students at the school. The standards were established to ensure that all students were challenged to reach their potential and contribute in meaningful ways to the community. The Kennedy Expected Schoolwide Learning Results (ESLRs) are to develop students who are

*Effective communicators who*
- Read, write, speak, and listen reflectively and critically for a variety of purposes and audiences
- Can perform in both collaborative and individual work environments
- Are exposed to strategies for resolving conflict

*Self-directed learners who*
- Gather and use information and demonstration strategies to solve problems
- Coordinate time management and organizational skills
- Create intellectual, artistic, practical, and physical products

*Effective users of technology who*
- Obtain, research, and organize information for personal, educational, and career purposes

*Involved citizens who*
- Examine and respond to social, health, and environmental issues
- Can identify the positive aspects of diversity

*Knowledgeable, effective candidates for the world of work who*

- Recognize the relationship between school and the workplace
- Set short- and long-term goals and work progressively toward their achievement
- Possess the requisite skills for the examination of a variety of career options

When asked about the performance standards at his school, one senior at Kennedy replied as follows:

> The ESLRs made it clear what I was expected to do. I knew in ninth grade that I had to create a portfolio that demonstrated my knowledge and skills in each of the areas. For example, I collected photos of my art projects, essays from English class, and computer design of a circuit board that I did in Electronics for the "create intellectual, artistic, practical, and physical products" requirement. I used the portfolio to graduate, but I also showed it during my apprenticeship job interview. The person interviewing me was very impressed that I had collected information from all my years of school and that I really could "recognize the relationship between school and the workplace." The ESLRs made me think beyond the individual class to what I was getting out of the school.

## INCLUSIVE EDUCATION AS PART OF SCHOOL REFORM

Prior to 1992, Kennedy High School had 28 students identified as having significant disabilities. These students, ages 14–22, attended one of three special day classes (SDCs). The focus of the education program for these students was community based. Students spent a significant part of their day in small groups traveling to shopping malls, parks, vocational development sites, and grocery stores. The remainder of the day's activities included cooking, functional academics, social skills development, and job preparation. Services and supports for these students were delivered in a traditional placement model. At this time, the students without disabilities attended classes for five to six 50-minute periods per day.

When the 1992–1993 school year began, the special education teachers decided to organize the SDCs according to the students' ages. The high school–age students (ages 14–18) were assigned to two teachers, and the transition-age students (ages 18–22) were also assigned to two teachers and had services coordinated by the third teacher. The education programs for these students changed significantly. The younger group was scheduled to spend more time performing school jobs and joining in extracurricular activities. The older group spent more time at jobsites and on community college campuses. By January 1993, a team including several Kennedy faculty members and staff from San Diego State University began discussions regarding changes in the special education service delivery model. The team developed a plan to include fully one student on a trial basis; the team received permission from the district administration to implement the plan in September 1993. In March 1993, however, a new student, Sarah, transferred into the school. Sarah's parents and her other IEP team members, including a district administrator, discussed enrolling her in five general education classes: English, biology, photography, math, and home economics.

Decisions for selecting these classes were based on the positive attitudes of the teachers involved as well as the relationship that each of them had with one special educator who assumed the leadership role in the negotiations. Within weeks, this special educator received positive feedback about Sarah's inclusion in the general education classes. At the same time, this teacher became increasingly frustrated trying to co-teach the SDC while providing the necessary supports and services to the general education teachers and Sarah. As a result, the team began planning for nine of the students identified as having severe disabilities to be fully included in general education academic classes. The other special education teacher responsible for high school–age students chose to maintain the more traditional, community-based structure.

The team expanded to include more general educators, and, after a summer of planning meetings and in-services, they successfully scheduled nine students identified with significant disabilities to attend general education classes. Individual schedules, reflecting typical grade-level schedules, were developed for each of the nine students for the 1993–1994 school year. None of the students attended the same class at the same time, although six of the students reported to the special educator for one class period per day to complete homework assignments. Students attended a variety of academic and elective classes, including art, English, film as literature, Spanish, math, physical education, chemistry, biology, geography, chorus, band, algebra, social studies, earth science, and photography.

The teacher who had maintained the traditional SDC applied for a position at another school because of his disagreement with the goals of inclusive education. He maintained that "students with severe disabilities need more functional skills training and more community-based instruction." The selection process for hiring a teacher to replace him included asking questions about inclusive education, collaborative team models, and strategies for building peer supports. The team was looking for a person who could answer the questions with enthusiasm and from experience. The school needed a teacher who understood both the "why" and the "how" of inclusive education. A new inclusion support teacher was hired at the beginning of the second semester. As a result, four additional students were scheduled to attend general education classes, leaving five students in the SDC by the end of the school year.

More planning and in-services were conducted during the summer of 1994, and, by the beginning of the fall semester, 35 general educators were committed to including students with disabilities in their classes. Kennedy's faculty voted to initiate a block/quarter schedule for the 1994–1995 school year. Moving to this schedule required that teachers acquire new skills in curriculum modifications because they had to engage students for more than 90 minutes. Training topics included experiential learning, cooperative groups, integrated curriculum, multilevel instruction, and collaboration skills. Teachers discovered that they were better prepared to meet the needs of all of their students. When the school year ended, all of the students with significant disabilities were learning in general education classes alongside their peers. Students were scheduled to attend classes according to their grade level, not according to their disability.

## Meet Jamie

Jamie is a twelfth grader at Kennedy High School. She has a well-developed sense of humor, and she enjoys rock music and science. She uses a wheelchair and is fairly independent in getting around the campus. She has little volitional movement in her legs and some spastic movement in both arms. Jamie's IQ score has been estimated to be in the range of mental retardation requiring extensive supports, and she has been diagnosed with cerebral palsy. Jamie communicates in two ways. First, she uses her eyes to answer yes-or-no questions. Second, Jamie can touch a communication device that plays prerecorded messages, such as "No way!" "My lap tray needs some adjustment," and "Thanks for the help." Jamie's attention span greatly increases when peers are present or when the radio is tuned to a favorite station.

During the first quarter of her senior year, Jamie was enrolled in photography, senior English, and science. Kennedy High School operates on a block system; thus, all students attend three classes per day. To be successful, Jamie requires special education supports and services in her general education classes. In her English class, a peer tutor assisted Jamie. During silent reading for the first 20 minutes of each period, she listened to required books on tape that a professional provided or that were recorded in the library. She kept a reading log to identify major events in the story and to record the number of pages to which she had listened. Her responsibilities were the same as those of other members of the class. She needed to be able to identify the major characters and the sequence of the story as well as understand the overall themes identified in the book. To do this, Jamie sequenced pictures that were photocopied from the book, created a collage of the major themes of the book, used her voice output device to play prerecorded messages during group time, and presented an outline version of an essay using Picture Communication Symbols (Mayer Johnson Co.).

## SPECIAL EDUCATION SUPPORTS

As the teachers' knowledge of inclusive education became more sophisticated, they formalized a process for supporting students with disabilities in their general education classes. Over the years, the forms have changed, and they are expected to continue to evolve. Many of the students at Kennedy require a curriculum that is adapted and modified for their individual abilities. The remainder of this section outlines the process that is used make such adaptations and modifications. Additional student examples can be found in Castagnera, Fisher, Rodifer, and Sax (1998).

Teachers at Kennedy consider three interrelated supports for every lesson: instructional and assistive technology, curriculum modifications, and specialized support staff (see Figure 1). Some students require considerable support in terms of curriculum and personnel, whereas others require less support. Each class and each lesson is unique, and teachers must plan accordingly. Overutilization of supports constitutes a restrictive intervention for the student and a situation in which the student learns little. Underutilization of these supports constitutes "dumping" and a situation in which the student may be set up to fail.

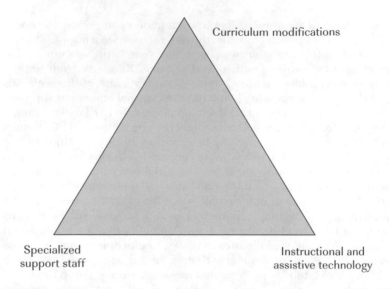

Figure 1.    Triangle of support for inclusive lesson planning.

## Instructional and Assistive Technology

Both instructional and assistive technology have been used to support students with and without disabilities in general education
classes. For example, many classes, especially English, make use of
computers. Students are encouraged to use the classroom computers to complete their assignments. In her English class, Jamie used a
computer with her peer tutor to complete her assignments. Jamie
responded to yes-or-no questions that Jamie and her peer tutors and
aides then turned into sentences and paragraphs. In terms of assistive
technology, Jamie used a voice output device, a customized lap tray,
and several switch-operated devices. The switch-operated devices
controlled battery-operated and electrically operated items such as a
water sprayer in a ceramics class and a tape recorder in choir. Other
students at Kennedy use assistive technology such as wheelchair ac-
cessories that enable them to carry books and materials from class
to class, visual aids that assist in reading and writing assignments,
and specialized software that features voice output and customized,
individualized settings that help students to process information
more effectively.

## Curriculum Modifications

Assignments and lesson plans are initially developed around the core curriculum and the content and performance standards for the class. When general education teachers provide multilevel instruction, adapting the lesson plan may not be necessary. This type of instruction allows the students a variety of ways to demonstrate knowledge while continuing to meet the requirements of the class. For example, the whole class may be responsible for creating a concept map of the plant unit in science. Jamie does not need any accommodations or modifications for this assignment. As the class members demonstrate their learning pictorially on a large piece of chart paper, Jamie participates by selecting pictures for the concept map by looking at the picture of her choice.

The amount and type of curriculum modification depend significantly on the lesson plan and the specific content of the class (see Table 1 for a summary of the range of modification options). As in the example of the concept map, the assignment is sometimes left as is for the student with an IEP.

Since the mid-1990s, with a focus on inclusive curriculum design (Jorgensen, 1998), more and more students are supported in this fashion. Some students, however, need accommodations to the lesson, even when they are expected to learn and follow the same lesson concepts. For example, teachers may enlarge the type or re-

Table 1.   Curriculum modification options

**Inclusive curriculum design**

Differentiated instruction—Provides for multiple ways of presenting and teaching information to students; when this type of instructional design is provided, the assignments remain unchanged

Accommodations—Increases the accessibility of the curriculum, including the use of large print, oral versions, and additional time for assignments

**Curriculum modification techniques**

Same, only less—Assignment remains the same, except that the number of items required is reduced

Streamline the curriculum—Assignment reduced in size to emphasize the key points

Same activity/infused objective—Assignment remains the same, but additional components are added

Curriculum overlapping—Assignment for one class may be completed in another class

quest a braille version of a paper. In addition, some students complete the same assignment but do less than other students. For example, on a multiple-choice test of U.S. history, the number of answers from which to choose for each question is reduced from five to two. If these modifications are not appropriate, teachers begin to streamline the curriculum. This means that the student is responsible for key aspects of the assignment but not necessarily the whole assignment. For example, when a research paper is assigned in English, Jamie completes an outline by using magazine pictures or Picture Communication Symbols. Her essay on *The Pearl* (Steinbeck, 1947) was completed by using Picture Communication Symbols with words. In addition, teachers may use the same activity with an infused objective. In Jamie's science class, she uses a switch to operate a voice output device and specialized equipment for standing at the laboratory tables with her partners. Finally, teachers overlap curriculums. Jamie and her peer tutor completed work for their ninth-grade geography class during word processing class, a one-term course requirement for all students.

## Specialized Support Staff

Students require varying amounts and types of specialized staff resources to be successful (see Table 2 for a summary of the range of personnel support options). Some students require full-time staff support. Special educators and aides provide this level of support. The staff member is often in proximity to the student and may assist with materials and supplies necessary to complete class assignments and group work. The staff member models cooperation, collaboration, and respect. This person also begins to facilitate relationships between students with and without disabilities, which in turn allows for less direct support and increased intermittent or part-time support. Full-time support is initially necessary for students with health requirements such as full-time oxygen or tube feedings and for students who need behavioral support.

As students learn the routines and customs of a class, the support staff begin to move to a part-time or intermittent support strategy. This level of support involves special educators' and aides' providing in-class assistance at predetermined times or checking in on classrooms on a regular basis. The staff person continues to maintain awareness of curriculum and assignments, and he or she may also provide assistance and direction to peer tutors as needed.

Table 2.    Personnel support options for students

Full-time staff support—Full-time support is provided by the staff in special education. The staff member remains seated in proximity to the student. Support staff may need to assist the student with materials and supplies needed to complete class assignments and group work. The staff provide a role model for cooperation, collaboration, acceptance, and respect for all.

Peer tutor—The peer tutor provides support to the student in a variety of ways. He or she may assist in mobility to and from class, carrying or remembering materials, taking notes, assisting with completing assignments, aiding facilitated communication, and serving as a role model for social interactions. The peer tutor may also participate in the development of support strategies. The peer tutor receives five elective credits for providing this support.

Part-time support—The support staff provide assistance to a student at a predetermined time or on a rotating basis. The staff member maintains an awareness of curriculum and assignments to encourage student productivity and completion of assignments and provides tutorial or organizational support.

Intermittent support—The support staff provide assistance in the classrooms on a daily or every-other-day basis to troubleshoot immediate challenges and/or to assist with surprise assignments or projects.

Natural support—This type of support is provided by students who are enrolled in the class. These students usually volunteer to provide support by taking notes, recording homework assignments, and so forth.

Supplemental support—Speech-language therapists, orientation and mobility specialists, physical therapists, and occupational therapists provide services in general education classrooms.

Peer tutors, also called peer facilitators or teacher's assistants, are also a common support option in secondary schools. Although these students do not replace the need for friends, tutors are often effective connectors to other students. At Kennedy, students can enroll in a teacher's assistant class. This elective class is open to all students, and tutors usually recruit their friends for future semesters. The peer tutors report to a specific teacher and complete a range of assignments, including providing support to students with disabilities who may be enrolled in the class. Peers often assist with mobility, notetaking, role modeling, and facilitating groups. The goal for these peer tutors is to facilitate the natural supports that are generically available in the class. Natural supports are supports to which any student in the class can gain access, including other students enrolled in the class who are not teacher's assistants or peer tutors.

Supplemental supports such as speech-language therapists, orientation and mobility specialists, physical therapists, and occupational therapists provide their services in general education classrooms. If this is not possible, services are provided at a time that is least disruptive to instruction.

## COMMUNICATION AMONG TEACHERS

A key factor in the success of providing educational services to all students is the ability of teachers to communicate effectively about students' academic and personal support needs, cooperate with lesson planning, and provide input to students' IEPs. Discussed next are several processes that have been developed to increase communication among teachers, including a student profile, an infused skills grid, an academic unit lesson plan or weekly assignment sheet, and a form on which teachers can provide input in a student's IEP.

### Student Profile

A student profile provides teachers with specific information about each student (see Figure 2). The general education teachers receive student profiles from special education teachers at the beginning of each term. The information in a student profile comes from family interviews, previous teachers, and others who know the student well. Using Jamie as an example, this form contains the following information:

- *Specific objectives for this class:* Jamie needs to arrive to class on time, have necessary materials, and ask for help when needed. The specific objectives are often taken from the IEP, but they are written in accessible language for all teachers.
- *Areas of strengths and interests:* Jamie loves anything related to music or science. A teacher may be able to use this information when designing projects or class activities.
- *Successful learning strategies and modifications or adaptations needed:* To complete written work, Jamie needs a larger grip to hold her pencil, and her paper must be anchored to her wheelchair tray. Her work must be enlarged, with additional spacing between words. This section of the form is useful for describing strategies as well as successful curriculum modifications.
- *Communication strategies:* Jamie answers yes-or-no questions and uses a Macaw Communication Board (Zygo Industries, Inc.) to communicate her wants and needs. This section includes any type

## Student Profile

Student name: Jamie Smith     Grade: 12     Student#: 0000

Parent/guardian: John and Jane Smith     Telephone: (123) 555-1212

**Quarter:** Second

**Class schedule**     Block 1: Academic block     Room: 227

Block 2: Electives     Room: 113

Block 3: Lunch     Room: Cafeteria

Block 4: Advisory     Room: 201

Block 5: Academic block     Room: 222

Advocate teacher: Mrs. Johnson

**Specific objectives for this class:** Jamie needs to arrive at class on time, have necessary materials, and ask for help when needed.

**Areas of strengths/interests:** Jamie loves anything related to music or science.

**Successful learning strategies and modifications/adaptations needed:** To complete written work, Jamie needs a larger grip to hold her pencil.

**Communication strategies:** Jamie answers yes-or-no questions and uses a communication board to communicate her wants and needs.

**Positive behavior support strategies:** Jamie becomes frustrated when she does not understand an assignment, so be sure she understands directions.

**Grading accommodations:** Jamie maintains a portfolio of completed assignments that is evaluated quarterly for grades and shared at her IEP meetings.

**Important family/health information:** It is important that Jamie be positioned properly in her wheelchair.

Figure 2.   Sample student profile form.

of augmentative and alternative communication supports that have been developed.

- *Positive behavioral support strategies:* Jamie becomes frustrated when she does not understand an assignment, so it is important to check for understanding after directions are given. Helpful hints about behavioral supports are important for teachers, especially when these hints have been successful in the past.
- *Grading accommodations:* Jamie maintains a portfolio of completed assignments that is evaluated quarterly for grades and shared at her IEP meetings. Students may require additional time on tests, oral versions of tests, or alternatives to tests.
- *Important family or health information:* It is important that Jamie be positioned properly in her wheelchair. Additional health information useful for teachers can be recorded in this section.

## Infused Skills Grid

Teachers will find the infused skills grid in Figure 3 useful in determining what and where to teach. This grid shows how functional skills can be infused into the daily routine of the student. Targeted skills generated from the student profile and family interviews are listed across the top right-hand side of the grid. Listed on the left side of the grid are the classes or environments that students attend throughout the day. A check mark is placed in each box that indicates a time period in which the skill will be addressed. For example, Jamie's family wanted her to learn how to dress herself, so a check mark was placed in the physical education (PE) column because this was a time period when she had opportunities to practice dressing skills at an appropriate time. Her family was also concerned about Jamie's learning to answer who, what, when, where, and why questions. This skill was addressed throughout all of her classes.

## Academic Unit Lesson Plan and Weekly Assignment Sheet

Teachers can organize their unit with the academic unit lesson plan (see sample in Figure 4). General education teachers indicate the major unit objectives, materials needed, instruction arrangements, projects and activities, and assessments. The completed form is then given to the inclusion support teacher, who in turn reviews each area and determines the level of modification or support needed. For example, Jamie's eleventh-grade English class was assigned *Of*

Student:  Jamie  
Age and grade:  17 years old, 12th grade  
Completed by:  
Date:  

## Infused basic skills

**Daily schedule**

| Daily schedule | Orientation and mobility | Time management | Communication "w" questions | Communication "wants and needs" | Computer word processing/spell-check | Reading: Sight vocabulary |
|---|---|---|---|---|---|---|
| Arrival | × | × | × | × |  | × |
| Photography | × | × | × | × | × | × |
| (Break) | × | × | × | × |  | × |
| Senior English | × | × | × | × | × | × |
| Lunch | × | × | × | × |  | × |
| Biology | × | × | × | × | × | × |
| Departure/Wednesday and Friday choir after school | × | × | × | × |  | × |
| Check here if the infused skill has been identified by → Family | × | × | × | × | × | × |
| Student | × | × | × | × | × | × |
| Peers | × | × | × |  |  |  |
| School | × | × | × | × | × | × |

Figure 3.   Sample infused skills grid.

**ACADEMIC UNIT LESSON PLAN FOR** *Of Mice and Men*

For <u>English</u> with <u>Ms. Bagg-Rizzo</u>  Beginning date <u>10/6</u> Ending date <u>10/17</u>
   Class        Teacher(s)

---

Major unit objective/expectations:

1. Students will evaluate their beliefs related to prejudice and diversity.
2. Students will learn about the plight of the migrant farm worker.
3. Students will learn about the Great Depression and the times in which Steinbeck wrote.

---

| Materials, books, media, worksheets, and so forth | Accommodations/modifications |
|---|---|
| 1. Copy of the short story "The Circuit"<br>2. Copy of the novel *Of Mice and Men*<br>3. Worksheets for each of the six chapters<br>4. Film adaptation of *Of Mice and Men*<br>5. Videotape camera<br>6. "Circle of Friends" worksheet | 1. Audiotape of the short story "The Circuit." A student in the class can be taped reading the story aloud.<br>2. Audiotape of the novel *Of Mice and Men*<br>3. Chapter summary worksheets and comprehension questions in yes-or-no format |
| Instruction arrangements<br>[*Describe time and opportunities for large group, small group, cooperative group, learning centers, individual activities, and nonclassroom instruction. Does instruction arrangement change from day to day?*]<br><br>1. Large-group instruction for introduction of the time period, Steinbeck, the Great Depression, and migrant farm workers<br>2. Small groups for "found poem" activity for "The Circuit"<br>3. Individual work on worksheets<br>4. Large-group presentation for trial of George; every student has a part in the trial<br>5. Arrangement will vary from day to day<br>6. Students design a "Circle of Friends" in small groups | Accommodations/modifications<br><br>1. Worksheets will be completed on the computer with the peer tutor.<br>2. Macaw Communication Board (Zygo Industries) will be programmed for part in trial.<br>3. "Circle of Friends" worksheet will be completed with Picture Communication Symbols (Mayer Johnson Co.). |

Figure 4.   Sample academic unit lesson plan.

*(continued)*

Figure 4.   *(continued)*

| Projects, supplemental activities, and homework | Accommodations/modifications |
|---|---|
| 1. "Found Poem" project on the short story "The Circuit"<br>2. Trial of George for killing Lennie<br>3. Homework: Worksheets for each chapter, study for part in trial, some reading of the novel at home | 1. Character worksheets (using Picture Communication Symbols [Mayer Johnson Co.]) will be completed for homework. |
| Assessment(s) and final products | Accommodations/modifications |
| 1. Trial presentation is videotaped.<br>2. Objective test<br>3. Evaluative essay | 1. Student participates in trial with speech output device.<br>2. Test will be read to student by a peer tutor. Answer choices will be limited to two. Student will mark answers on answer sheet with highlighting marker.<br>3. The outline for the essay will be completed by using the computer, and a pictorial collage will be made to represent the theme of each section of the outline. |

*Mice and Men* (Steinbeck, 1938). The English teacher designed the weeklong unit to focus on prejudice, diversity, migrant farm workers, and the Great Depression. She selected a variety of printed materials, a videotape, and related activity sheets, organizing instruction into individual assignments, small-group work, whole-class participation, and student performances. Students in the class read related poetry and stories, completed homework assignments, and conducted a mock trial based on the novel. Assessments for this unit included the videotaped trial, an objective test, and a final essay. All of this information is recorded on the left side of the lesson plan form. Using the modification process described previously, the inclusion support teacher completes the right side of the form, suggesting appropriate accommodations and adaptations as necessary.

The general education teacher completes the Weekly Assignment Sheet on a weekly basis (see Figure 5). Teachers use this form to communicate events—for example, tests, assignments, projects, and other activities. Sharing this information makes it easier for teachers to obtain in advance materials that need to be modified. They

ASSIGNMENTS

WEEK OF:
10 / 6

Teacher's name: _Ms. Bagg-Rizzo_

Student's name: _Jamie_

|  | Tests | Worksheets | Projects | Other |  |
|---|---|---|---|---|---|
| Monday |  | x |  | x | _Begin Of Mice and Men (OMEM) Chs. 1 & 2. Complete worksheets._ |
| Tuesday |  | x | x | x | _Continue OMEM Chs. 3 & 4 worksheets, intro trial, and assign parts._ |
| Wednesday |  | x | x | x | _Finish OMEM Chs. 5 & 6 worksheets, practice trial._ |
| Thursday |  |  |  | x | _Practice trial, complete graphic organizer._ |
| Friday |  |  |  | x | _Trial_ |

Comments: _OMEM test Monday and introduction of evaluative essay._

Please return this form to _Ms. Rodifer_ 's box. Thanks!

Figure 5.   Sample weekly assignment sheet.

attach copies of the original test or assignment to the form, and the inclusion support teacher makes the necessary modifications.

## Teacher Input to the Individualized Education Program

General education teachers play an important role in the IEP process for the students whom they support in their classes. By completing the IEP input form (see Figure 6) at the end of each term, teachers are able to share their perspectives of student successes and areas

---

Teacher ___Ms. Bagg-Rizzo___    Student ___Jamie Smith___

Class ___English___    Block __3__    Date __10/6__

***Please return to ___Ms. Rodifer___ Thank you!!!

When completing the following form, please consider relevant social, organizational, and communication/language areas in addition to academic areas specific to your class and class activities.

**1. What do you consider the student's strengths to be?**

Jamie is always willing to do anything I ask her to do. She is always the first to volunteer. If the peer tutor tells her to give another person a chance, she gets mad. Jamie is very considerate of the climate in the classroom. If she comes into class late, she now goes to her seat area quietly rather than needing to greet everyone.

**2. What skills do you see the student learning in your class?**

Jamie has shown significant growth in her ability to answer my questions during book talks and any other general knowledge questions I ask her. She is doing a much better job of accepting constructive criticism and asking for assistance when she needs it.

**3. Indicate the areas of need that you think are the most critical to the student's success in your class:**

Jamie concentrates best when she works with a female peer tutor. I have found this to be true also when the students are working in groups. Jamie likes to flirt with the young men rather than complete the assignment given.

---

Figure 6.    Sample individualized education program input form.

of need. For example, the English teacher noticed that during book talks, Jamie learned to accept constructive criticism better when she heard it from both her teacher and her friends. Receiving input from all of her teachers provided a more complete picture of how Jamie was succeeding in a variety of environments.

## STUDENTS' VOICES

As we were writing this chapter about the changes at Kennedy High School, we decided to talk with some students from the school and give voice to their beliefs. We asked a number of students to explain their understanding of the reasons for inclusive education. The students responded simply that students with disabilities "are people who are entitled to a quality education" and defined *quality* as access to general education classes. In this vein, a number of students made statements such as "All students have rights," "People are people," "All means all," and "They deserve access to the same opportunities." One senior was more philosophical. He said, "I have the right to experience human diversity in my school." In his explanation of this statement to the class, he expressed his concern that lack of contact between people with and without disabilities would only lead to further segregation and discrimination.

A ninth grader, Wayne, told a story about a peer with significant behavior challenges who attended his Spanish class. He said that when Santiago first started at the school, he would not even come on the campus. Santiago stayed in a general education class for only about 30 of the 90 minutes that he was at school, and he sometimes would yell, hit himself, and run out of the room. Santiago became a well-known member of the class. He stays for the entire period, his Spanish has improved, and he has great relationships with his peers. Wayne added that he has learned to be a good role model for Santiago because, otherwise, Santiago will start "acting up, not know how to stop, and end up getting in a lot of trouble." This "two-way social learning," as a junior described it, was identified across grade levels. Several students indicated that they had learned to behave in class by watching the effect of their negative behavior on their peers with disabilities.

One junior summed up her understanding of inclusive education with a simple statement: "I see my younger sister, who has disabilities, in a whole new light. I have learned what I was afraid of." A senior in an English class shared his impressions:

> My general education has been option filled; I have had the opportunity to learn from lots of people, both teachers and students. I have learned to see the world in new ways, partly because of the way Jamie sees the world.

## CONCLUSIONS

A teacher from another school district visited Kennedy High School, and she spoke with us about her day of observation. She was amazed and a bit dismayed at how different Kennedy was from the schools in her district. Seeing students with significant disabilities truly participating in academic classes; hearing teachers address all students as their own; and feeling the camaraderie among students, teachers, and administrators clarified for her how far her school still had to go to become inclusive. We reminded her that every school has different starting points and changes at an individual pace. We also reminded her that we still had a number of issues about which we were concerned and wanted to address. From our perspective, these challenges include the following:

1. *Continuing to focus on the supports and services that ensure student success:* As the student population becomes move diverse and their needs change, we believe in maintaining our commitment to the inclusion of all students.
2. *Supporting neighboring local high schools as they develop inclusive education programs:* One of our concerns is the number of families who want to move into the Kennedy High School district so that their children will have an inclusive educational experience. We understand the families' desires but are concerned that our school population will increase above the capabilities of the staff and that natural proportions will be violated. We believe that more schools must redesign their service delivery models to provide inclusive educational opportunities to the students in their geographic area.
3. *Continuing to develop content area instruction units that respect individual students' strengths while addressing our standards and ESLRs:* We believe that all students can reach high standards

and that curriculum, instruction, and assessments must be adapted, modified, and accommodated to reach this goal.

4.  *Creating opportunities for high school students to talk about their experiences in school, including their perspectives of inclusive education:* We believe that the curriculum must reflect the range of human experiences and that students need many opportunities to derive meaning from these experiences.

5.  *Maintaining support for professional development experiences and fostering connections with our respected critical friends:* We believe that more teachers need to receive their preservice training in inclusive schools and that teachers need to participate in continuing professional development activities. In addition, we would like to see these experienced teachers provide mentorship to student teachers and newly hired teachers. Regardless of where the starting points are or the pace at which changes occur, ongoing reflection and reevaluation ensure that the needs of students, teachers, administrators, and community members will continue to be met.

6

# John Q. Adams High School

## A Pilot Project Takes Shape

Caren Sax
Douglas Fisher
Lois Chappell
Lyn Pratt

"Adams High School? It doesn't seem to be anyone's first choice of where to teach, but once you start teaching here, you never want to leave." Teachers, administrators, and support staff all respond similarly when asked why they teach at John Q. Adams High School (hereinafter referred to as Adams). A certain mystique seems to exist at this high school; understanding its unique culture was a major factor in determining how inclusive education fits into the school's restructuring plans.

Outsiders often have difficulty in interpreting the school's culture, and even new teachers admit that "it takes a while to figure out how things work" in the school. While listening to teachers in the faculty lounge, one may hear a range of conversation topics. Teachers from the business department may be talking with parents or community members about developing local business partnerships. English and history teachers may be discussing the school's latest technology acquisitions and sharing tips for gaining access to the new resources available on the Internet. Still others may be planning for the next faculty happy hour. Just as likely, many teachers are brainstorming about specific students who need extra help to survive the next term. People involve themselves in each other's lives, which may be one of the reasons why the average length of service of the staff at Adams is about 15 years.

Given the large size and entrepreneurial management style of the school, new projects at Adams typically target individual departments or specific groups of students. As described in the next section, Adams secured funding for a number of projects in the mid- to late 1990s. Rather than compete with these projects, Adams designed a pilot program to address the needs of students with disabilities by expanding the focus of major restructuring efforts. Although making Adams an inclusive school by combining this goal with other restructuring efforts placed the inclusive education goal at risk of becoming "just another project," this approach made sense within the culture of the school. As with other districts that have used pilot programs to "sell" the idea of inclusive education, Adams serves as a model for other stakeholders within and outside the district.

## HISTORY AND BACKGROUND

Adams faculty and staff tend to maintain as much autonomy and independence as possible. When its school district initiated site-based management, Adams readily adopted this approach, which enhanced its ability to govern itself. Teachers saw the approach as an opportunity to have more input into how the school operated, and administrators knew that this type of group process was essential for initiating refocusing efforts. One of the strategies that the school used to implement site-based management was engaging the faculty in shared decision making. Shared decision making at Adams is an inclusive process that allows all stakeholders to be represented in making decisions that positively affect student achievement. The site-governance team focuses on issues such as portfolio and senior exhibition, career paths, community service, alternative scheduling, and technology integration. Task groups are commissioned with the power and resources to research and develop new policies and practices. The administration knew that, for change to occur, all stakeholders needed to feel ownership of what was being designed and implemented. The ultimate aim was to create a community of learners experiencing new professional roles.

As a guide for designing schoolwide goals that are consistent with the values of its faculty and administrators, Adams abides by the following school district mission statement: "It is the mission of [our district] to educate all students in an integrated setting to become responsible, literate, thinking, and contributing members of a multicultural society through excellence in teaching and learning" (John Q. Adams School District, n.d.). Based on this statement, Adams staff set goals in the following areas: improving student learning, improving teaching, enhancing integration and diversity, and enhancing shared decision making and community involvement. In addition, the school clarified its commitment to the following core values:

1.  Total community and parental involvement in the education process
2.  Diligent promotion of understanding of the gifts of diverse groups
3.  Maximum effort to increase attendance
4.  Aggressive provisions for a safe learning environment that encourages students' regular attendance, sense of self-worth, and pride in the school
5.  Commitment to providing a variety of rich educational experiences

6.   Increased recognition and acknowledgment of all student and staff accomplishments

Adams High School, housed on 57 acres in a culturally diverse neighborhood in southeast San Diego, enrolls approximately 2,500–3,000 students in any given year (see Table 1 for demographic information). The campus has more than 100 classrooms. Although the area of San Diego where Adams is located is known for its high poverty rate (54% of area residents were living below the federally defined poverty level in 1996 [School accountability report card, 1996]), drugs, and gang activity, the school boasts a rich and harmonious educational environment. Both a housing development in the area and the school opened in 1962. The neighborhood and the school have grown by a proportionately equal amount since the school opened its doors to 1,200 students that first year.

Thirteen elementary schools and three middle schools feed into Adams, which was renamed "The Center for Technology and Pacific Rim Studies" in 1994. Supplemental grant funding for Adams has totaled more than $2 million since 1994, including a large National Science Foundation award for expanding the school's use of technology. The school faculty has worked to restructure the way in which they deliver instruction to meet the vision of the "new California high school" as described in the California High School Task Force (1992) document *Second to None*. Themes of this document feature curriculum paths, powerful teaching and learning, accountability and assessment, student support, restructuring the school, and developing new professional roles for school staff. Based on this document, as well as on school change research, Adams designed five curricular paths: science; engineering; hospitality, tourism, and recreation; world languages and communication; and aeronautics and automotive transportation. The paths integrate required and elective courses, which are designed to help students plan for their lives after high

Table 1.   Student demographics at John Q. Adams High School

*Racial and ethnic composition:* 46% Pilipino, 25% African American, 17% Hispanic, 7% Caucasian, 3% Southeast Asian American, 2% Pacific Islander

*Describing the school in educational terms:* 19% of students are identified as gifted or talented; 10% have IEPs; 6% have limited proficiency in English and a primary language other than English, representing 11 different languages

*Economic status:* 54% of students qualify for free or reduced lunch

school. According to Adams students who were asked about their postgraduation plans, 60% planned to attend either a 2- or a 4-year institution, 20% expected to enlist in the military, and 20% indicated that they would go to work or attend a technical or trade school. Each career path offers opportunities for students to direct their learning toward any of these destinations.

Teachers and administrators at Adams have been well aware of the reading impairments of students entering their high school. In the late 1990s, reading tests administered to incoming ninth and tenth graders showed that 75% were 2 or more years below grade level in reading skills. Disaggregated data revealed that African American students fell behind the school population in a number of categories. They had lower overall grade point averages, tested at lower reading levels, and were suspended twice as often as other students. Scores on math tests improved during the late 1990s; the proportion of all students earning a "C" or better in math increased from 59% in 1994–1995 to 65% in 1996–1997. Disaggregated data show that Hispanic students scored lowest in this area.. To address these intensive needs, faculty are investigating teaching styles, grading policies, reading levels of textbooks, and gender-related and psychological barriers to certain subject areas. More effective strategies and interventions must be initiated, particularly for African American and Hispanic students. Despite the low scores, which typically lead to other serious issues (e.g., failure in more courses, increased number and magnitude of behavior problems, lower graduation rates), additional schoolwide interventions have reduced the dropout rates for all ethnic groups significantly.

Adams's school governance committee involves school staff, students, and family members, as well as community and business partners. The committee meets monthly to discuss a specific topic of schoolwide concern (e.g., student–teacher ratios, school day structure, student achievement). Although parent involvement is always a challenge at the high school level, efforts to engage families in Adams's activities have met with some success. A new Parent Center was designed to welcome families to the school, and a Parent Institute was held, in which more than 90 parents participated. The Pilipino Parents' Association encouraged more families to become active in school issues and helped to organize evening language classes.

Both informal and formal business partners were also active in the school via a Business Education Advisory Group, which included representatives from local industry, corporate, and military organizations. Adams has always been interested in pursuing partnerships with local universities and community businesses. For example, San Diego State University places student teachers and interns at Adams on a regular basis, and the university has also been instrumental in helping to develop expertise in technology integration. Business and community partners have been involved in the implementation of the career paths by providing expertise in curriculum development, apprenticeship opportunities, and summer internships.

Although shared decision making is a priority at Adams, all major budget decisions remain at the district level. Adams receives categorical funds for many programs, including Gifted and Talented Education, Education Consolidation and Improvement Act, Titles I and II, special education, magnet, core curriculum, dropout prevention, and a number of miscellaneous grants. These funds help purchase equipment and supplies and pay the hours for tutoring and aides.

Support for students identified as "at risk for school failure" or, as members of the school say, "at promise for school success," also concerns faculty and staff. Adams offers tutoring (before and after school and during lunch); Saturday school; off-track and parallel courses; extended day classes (advancement via individual determination [AVID] and reading strategies); summer school; the Student Support Center (addressing students' and families' emotional and social needs); peer mediation; and focus groups that discuss pregnancy, drugs, violence, and similar issues.

## CHRONOLOGY OF CHANGE

Beginning in 1993, Adams began its refocusing plan for becoming a total school magnet. The administration urged teachers and other stakeholders to participate in a number of retreats to identify and build on what was working at the school while restructuring to become a "more dynamic institution that would better serve the needs of all of its students." The original refocusing plan included discussion and planning in the areas of student achievement, effective teaching plans, curriculum, and evaluation. During the first year of the program, ninth graders were invited to participate in a "tech prep" wheel of introductory world at work courses that were developed jointly by the industrial technology, consumer and family studies, and business departments. This rotation of classes was designed to help students set education and career goals. The plan called for every ninth grader to be enrolled in an introductory career program by the fourth year of the magnet expansion.

Talking about change and implementing change can be worlds apart at a school with a staff the size of Adams's, which has more than 120 credentialed teachers. Although planning continues, paths have been established and reestablished, and perceptions of many at the school indicate that not all students know about career paths and not all teachers know their roles in guiding the students into the world of work. Major efforts have focused on improving reading and math scores, but reorganizing traditional departments into interdisciplinary teams that offer thematic courses according to career paths still seems somewhat vague. For their annual action plan in 1996, stakeholders collaborated to identify content standards, learner outcomes, benchmark indicators, and performance expectations to assess curriculum alignment, instruction strategies, and consistency of delivery across grade levels and subjects (Jacobs, 1997; Tomlinson, 1995; Tucker & Codding, 1998).

The staff development plan is an extension of the site-shared decision-making process. A committee including both certified and classified staff designs a plan yearly. For the teaching staff, the focus has been on instruction strategies (e.g., cooperative learning). Integrating technology and strategies to reduce class size were also priorities in the late 1990s. All teachers use personal computers connected to an internal listserv (a computer database) as well as to the Internet. Training has been facilitated by the use of triads (one content expert with two novices), building on the expertise of staff as well as the San Diego State University faculty. In an effort to make a more informed decision on the use of alternative scheduling, several biology and math classes experimented with using a block schedule, which produced positive results for many students. The staff are still divided on whether to adopt a new schedule, although a number of teachers continue to implement a block schedule in their classrooms. Teachers have also received training in the use of cognitive, or peer, coaching to support one another in how they provide instruction to students. Approximately a dozen teachers have completed the full training and comment on how its use helps to remove the feeling of isolation that is all too common.

Another catalyst for change at Adams is the use of consultants. "Outsiders" often clarify needs and concerns and help the faculty to refocus their efforts. The redesign of the reading program is an example of a successful use of consultants. A group of teachers already engaged in addressing the needs of less fluent readers met with a consultant to plan a systematic approach to the problem. They designed a reading course for students reading 2 or more years below ninth-grade level that included a range of literacy strategies (see Table 2). When teachers tested eighth graders at the feeder schools during their last semester, they identified approximately 300 students who were reading well below grade level.

Adams notified all families of incoming ninth graders about the new reading course. The reading course was designed to accelerate rapidly the reading rates and comprehension of both fiction and non-fiction material. The goal was to prepare students for successful completion of secondary-level academic work by addressing their reading needs. Major elements of the course included extensive reading and vocabulary development, comprehension strategies, and inductive strategies for content. Teachers also worked with students to set goals and learn how to evaluate their own progress. The course emphasized at-home reading in addition to the reading course at school. Students set goals of how many books they would read during each 6-week period and then reported in logs as they completed each one. Families were asked to support at least 30 minutes of reading per night. From the results of testing after 1 year, intensive reading instruction greatly accelerated the reading skill levels of the targeted students. Interviews with students indicated that recreational reading was rare and that, generally, students did not enjoy reading. As a result, more resources are being used to provide in-class libraries and high-interest, low-difficulty books. Collaboration among administration, faculty, and families contributed to the success of these efforts.

## WHERE DO STUDENTS WITH DISABILITIES FIT?

Historically, Adams has maintained a special education department. Services are provided for students identified under the California definition of learning handicaps, social and emotional disabilities, and severe disabilities. Until 1996, transition services for students ages 18–22 with significant disabilities used the campus as a base.

Table 2.    Literacy strategies

## Read, Write, Pair, Share

Students read a selected passage silently and write their initial reactions. The teacher then pairs the students to give them an opportunity to share what they have written and what they thought and felt about the passage. Students then discuss their responses in a larger group or with the whole class. This sequence can be repeated with the teacher reading the passage aloud the second time. Students write additional reactions to the selection, share with a different partner, and then discuss with the whole group again.

## Read-Alouds

Shared reading experiences in which teachers read to students or in which students read to other students provide opportunities to discuss background knowledge that relates to the reading selection. Read-alouds draw students into the literary experience, create interest, and motivate students to investigate related content areas.

## Concept Maps

Concept maps help students to organize prior knowledge and construct new understandings as they create a spatial representation of ideas and concepts. Concept maps can be used to introduce new content areas, gauge student progress during instruction, or assess students' understanding at the end of a unit.

## Prereading Strategies

Questioning students prior to their reading a book encourages them to tap into background knowledge that might be relevant to the new concepts. Questions are often open ended and encourage students to make free associations. By using this strategy, teachers can more easily identify both accurate and inaccurate knowledge that students bring to the new context.

## During-Reading Strategies

Questions asked during reading help teachers monitor students' comprehension. Teachers may ask content- and process-related questions and provide organizational guides that help students to focus on specific aspects of the material. Both teachers and students can be responsible for generating questions.

## After-Reading Strategies

These strategies include questions that help students to remember as well as to comprehend what they have read. As a result, students review the content, identify new understandings, and integrate this knowledge into their personal experience.

These students, however, spent the majority of their time in the community. The school district provided transition services via the Mobilizing Education and Transition Resources Off-Campus (METRO) program. Supported and paid for by the district, most of the METRO classes are located on community college campuses and in storefronts. Students may work, attend higher education classes, participate in community activities, and begin to help design their post–high school careers. Efforts to connect students and their families to adult agencies for supported employment and supported living services are under way to ease this transition.

Special educators have provided services to high school–age students in a number of ways. Many teachers of students identified with learning disabilities either collaborated or consulted with other teachers in general education classrooms to meet the educational needs of their students. Other teachers used special education–only classrooms and organized students by their categorical labels. These self-contained classes had fewer students and often implemented a parallel curriculum. Few of the students with significant disabilities attended general education classes, and, when they did, they typically attended elective courses (e.g., physical education, nutrition or cooking, art). More often these students participated in community-based instruction and were provided functional skills and vocational experiences. Students identified as having social and emotional disabilities spent most of their time in a "bungalow" classroom (i.e., a nonpermanent structure). The special education staff divided their classes and tasks based on curriculum or departments. Other job responsibilities, such as serving as department chair or on hiring committees and conducting 3-year reviews and individualized education program (IEP) and individualized transition plan meetings, were divided among the resource specialists.

The climate of special education began changing when Adams was identified as a project site for a California Department of Education research, development, and demonstration (RD&D) initiative. Teachers, parents, and students completed surveys to help identify what was working and what could be improved within the service delivery model. Results from these surveys supported the need for changing procedures in the service delivery model to support all students more effectively. Discussions grew more intense as the stakeholders asked more difficult questions.

One particularly memorable meeting scheduled during that period represented the shift in thinking about how the special education department was determining placements and providing supports for students with more significant disabilities. The following is a re-creation of some of the dialogue from that meeting:

*Jorge:*    We're here today to talk about ideas for breaking out of our categorical model. So, how can we redistribute resources according to students' needs rather than according to their disability label? I think some of us are already experimenting with this approach. For example, I am supporting Margarita, who has very significant disabilities, in the business computer class. She has an expanded keyboard that we have connected to one of the computers, and she works on simplified versions of the assignments. Several other students labeled with learning disabilities are enrolled in the class, whom I also support. Anne, the resource teacher, met with us early on to describe IEP goals and the accommodations that each student might require to participate and succeed in the class. I've been working more closely with Ms. Anderson, who teaches the class, to share other course responsibilities. I'm pretty good on the computer myself, so it's easy to think of ways for us to maximize our resources.

*Shirin:*    A number of us have also tried team teaching with general educators, and we discovered that the combination of content expertise and skills in designing individual learning strategies leads to better instruction for all students. Of course, not all of the teachers are comfortable with that arrangement. Some of them still treat us as if we were their aides, while others are seeing us as peers. We need to demonstrate our skills in not only modifying and adapting curriculum but also showing them how our skills really do complement theirs. I may not be an expert in biology, but I can design roles and responsibilities for students to perform experiments in cooperative learning groups. I'm really good at designing outlines and graphics of course materials that highlight the main concepts. I'm sure that more than just the "labeled" students could benefit from that!

*Nancy:*   Wait a minute. This all sounds good for our students with learning disabilities, but what about the kids in Room 903? Surely you don't expect us to change diapers when we're in English class? And what about that kid who needs the oxygen tank? Don't we have to draw the line somewhere?

*Jorge:*   Careful now, Nancy. Let's not have that old argument again. We're all professionals here; we need to figure out how to use our expertise and our training to provide all students with the best instruction that we possibly can. We all need to learn more about the general education curriculum and become more familiar with the framework for each of the subject areas. I know that we can influence the instruction here; we owe it to all of the students.

Clearly, everyone had more to learn about what was possible, and further staff development in these areas was necessary. The conversation had been difficult; but at least the fears, misunderstandings, and questions had been expressed and could be addressed. Although no major changes were agreed on at that time, teachers and aides were willing to take initial steps into this uncharted territory and continue to explore new options for improving the way things were done. They at least walked away from the meeting agreeing to explore new partnerships with their general education colleagues. The momentum was building.

By the second year of the state project, significant changes were initiated. Students identified with learning disabilities were included in general education classes, significantly reducing the number of parallel classes. Noncredit courses were still available, but they were restructured and opened to students with and without disabilities. The resource specialists teamed with general educators for sheltered instruction, serving special education students and transitioning bilingual students, particularly in science and English. Many students with more significant disabilities attended core academic classes, initially with full-time support, as both special and general education teachers increased their comfort levels in these new situations. Collaboration and consultation occurred more regularly between special and general educators in all subject areas, especially in academic core classes. One aide provided support in the computer math lab. Others supported students in core academic classes as well as in electives. The special education staff started to merge support services, giving classroom teachers one point of contact for all of the students with IEPs in their classrooms. Resource specialists provided study skills training to any student in need of those competencies, regardless of whether he or she had been labeled with a disability. During this training, students learn effective strategies for reading and studying a content area textbook, taking notes, and reading hand-outs in preparation for a class examination. Students also practice content skills, which may include the use of specific tools, equipment, and measuring devices. In addition, students become more adept at participating and communicating in the classroom. (See Table 3 for a list of study skills topics.)

Merging expertise, supports, and interests opened countless opportunities for students, as well as teachers, in the special education department. Students participated in programs that had been available but to which they had had minimal access, including apprenticeship programs, regional occupational programs, and other work opportunity programs. The special education department opened a computer lab and began a career development class. Both of these opportunities were available to all students. As the career path committees formed, special educators were represented in each

Table 3.   Study skills

To develop more effective study skills, students may work on the following topics:
- Identifying interests, talents, and learning styles and learning how to use them better
- Linking attitudes to success in the classroom
- Creating time management strategies
- Developing positive studying behaviors
- Learning to deal with distractions
- Listening more effectively
- Understanding how textbooks are organized
- Expanding vocabulary
- Identifying the strategies that are most effective with students
- Overcoming test anxiety
- Preparing for tests
- Test-taking strategies
- Learning memorization techniques
- Learning how to outline textual materials
- Taking notes from lectures, videotapes, overheads, and group sessions
- Writing skills, including proofreading, editing, and using different styles
- Using reference materials
- Overcoming the fear of speaking in front of the class

path. Similarly, as senior portfolios were phased in, all teachers received lists of seniors to monitor, regardless of categories, departments, or labels, once again merging supports across the board.

By the end of the state funding cycle, services were better coordinated, including Title I, sheltered, and special education. Students were enrolled in classes based on need rather than on whether they had been labeled with a disability, and the study skills program continued to offer tutoring and extra support to any student who could benefit from the focused instruction. Lunchtime tutoring was implemented to coach students referred by any teacher. Furthermore, students with significant disabilities were scheduled for classes like everyone else, according to their grade-level requirements. The day that the special education staff sat down to fill out schedule cards was a milestone at Adams and signified that there was no turning back! Students with IEPs would be attending their classes on the first day of school as assigned. No more visiting occasionally, trying out for the class, or testing the class for comfort; the student had an assigned seat that indicated membership as a typical student in the class.

Strategies for communicating with general education teachers also had to be reexamined. Typically, one of the special educators or aides is the primary contact for a particular teacher. Each situation must be determined by the needs of the student and the comfort levels of the parties involved. Communication in any form is essential. Regardless of whether the communication is written, verbal, intensive, or minimal, it must be consistent and available. In addition, peer tutors were available both during and after classes to help make the whole schedule work successfully. Students assisted with curriculum adaptations as well as with social interactions. Peer tutors were also essential for identifying classrooms that were good matches for specific students. Special educators began planning for students entering Adams from the feeder junior high and middle schools, conducting tours and presentations for students to help them design schedules for the following year. Seniors were paired with the new students to help with their transition to high school. The stage was set for the next phase of change.

## INFUSING AN UNDERSTANDING
## OF DISABILITY INTO THE CURRICULUM

Forward thinkers in the area of restructuring, inclusive schools agree that special educators have to step outside their "field" to address the larger community of students, teachers, administrators, and community members. At Adams, the special educators' first step required looking beyond the specific disability category. The next step was to address issues beyond special education. We used to think that teaching functional skills to students who were labeled "mentally retarded," "multiply handicapped," or "autistic" was adequate for them to succeed as adults. We learned that if we did not teach people with and without disabilities how to interact and how to recognize the skills and talents that each had to offer, then their prospects for success as adults were limited. Teachers at Adams had the opportunity via the RD&D project to interact with many of their colleagues from neighboring high schools. They learned about inclusive curriculum design, adaptations, modifications, and personal supports. As they worked to create an inclusive school, however, based on the success of the original pilot project, the teachers noticed that many of their typical students did not understand why students with disabilities were enrolled in their classes. Sure, students saw people who were different from themselves, and maybe they even occasionally interacted with people from different backgrounds. Teachers wanted more than that, however; they were looking for students who understood diversity as a resource. Teachers began to ask themselves, "How different will it be when students who respect and value individual differences run the world?" As they contemplated that question, they realized that their curriculum needed to reflect the range of human experiences. As a result, the teachers at Adams began infusing social justice issues into the curriculum.

Consider the following example of a presentation in a high school "family and child development" class:

*Teacher:*  What percentage of your graduating class is likely to become doctors?

*Students:*  Maybe 3%.

*Teacher:*  What percentage of your graduating class is likely to become lawyers?

*Students:*  Maybe 6%.

*Teacher:*  What about teachers?

*Students:*  [*Growing impatient*]: Lots!

*Teacher:*   Well, if you are similar to the national average, about 12% will become teachers. Here's one more question. What percentage of your graduating class is likely to become parents of children with disabilities?

*Students:*   [*Silence*]

*Teacher:*   Easily 20%. How much preparation do you have for that likelihood? [*After some discussion, the following activity is initiated.*] I'd like you to take out a piece of paper and write a letter to friends who just gave birth to a child with a disability. What would you say to them? [*Teacher allows time for the students to write.*] Now, write down what you would like to hear from your friends if you or your spouse just gave birth to a child with a disability. [*Students and teacher continue to compare and contrast what they might say to others versus what they would expect to hear, as well as what information and resources they might need to deal effectively with the situation. Teachers may want to invite parents of children with disabilities to speak to the class about their experiences.*]

Infusing information about disability issues into the general education curriculum provides a holistic approach for changing attitudes and behavior. Traditionally, lessons about disability were limited to an annual event such as "Disability Awareness Day." At such a time, students typically "try on" a disability for a short period of time to get a glimpse of what it feels like, for example, to be blind (by using a blindfold), to use a wheelchair, to have fine motor difficulties (by wearing several socks on their hands while trying to use a screwdriver), or to have a learning disability (by trying to read or write text reflected in a mirror). Unfortunately, unless the activities are debriefed in such a way as to also highlight what people can accomplish given the appropriate supports and adaptations, many students walk away from the experience saying, "I'm sure glad I don't have a disability. I don't know how they do anything!" The following entry from one student's journal demonstrates that other lessons can be learned when the activities are set up differently.

Although there are many changes that have occurred within me, the most noticeable one that has affected me personally is the feeling of

NOT feeling sorry. There was a time when I would look at a person with a disability and say they can do so much more if they were not blind or paraplegic or "confined to that wheelchair." I now realize that being blind or paraplegic does not mean that a person is dead, and I also realize that there is no one who is confined to anything but merely using a wheelchair. Although the society that we live in does not share my views, I feel it is up to each and every one of us to share our knowledge with those who are ignorant, like we were at the beginning of the semester. I realize this sounds idealistic, but the only way I can prove this to anyone is to lead by example. In the past few weeks, I have found myself stopping people from saying "that cripple" or "the retard." The changes that have been made in my way of thinking as a result of these activities will stay with me throughout my life, especially when I become a medical doctor.

As teachers infuse information about disability throughout the curriculum, they reinforce the idea that disability is part of the human experience. Some of the following activities have been conducted in general education classes at Adams, as well as at other high schools, as alternatives to the "disability of the week" approach. Designing these activities to fit naturally into the curriculum is an assignment for student teachers and interns who are earning credentials in special education and teacher education at San Diego State University. These activities are sure to become a great resource for general education teachers who, like the English teacher from Chapter 4, did not grow up with students with disabilities.

## World History

During Ms. Wallinsky's unit on World War II, the juniors learned some painful lessons about the Holocaust. Although some of them were familiar with the stories of how many Jews were killed and how other groups were also persecuted, most were shocked to learn about the experiments that were done on people with disabilities to perfect the execution strategies (Friedlander, 1995). The special educator, Mrs. Hayes, teamed with Ms. Wallinsky to present this information. The "I heard a rumor" activity (see Figure 1) was used as an introduction to the lesson. A variation on the children's "telephone game," in which one child tells another child what was heard, and then that child tells another child, and so forth, the first message inevitably changes meaning. The "I heard a rumor" activity begins by sending six students out of the room. The class is told what will happen and that their responsibility is to listen for the changes that

## "I Heard a Rumor . . . " Lesson Plan

**Overview:** Rumors have a way of becoming something that everyone believes is true. Unfortunately, many rumors hurt people. In this activity, students see how easily information can change over time and how it is influenced by people's knowledge and experience.

**Objectives:**
- To demonstrate how and why rumors are born
- To isolate particular breaks in communication
- To demonstrate how personal bias creates distortion
- To provide practice in objective listening

**Activity** (a variation on the Telephone Game):
1. Choose six students, and ask them to leave the room.
2. Choose another student in the class to be the Rumormonger, and tell that student a rumor (see examples listed below).
3. Student #1 enters the room. The Rumormonger reads the rumor to that student. Each of the other students who were asked to leave the room reenters the room one at a time to be told the rumor by the student who preceded him or her into the room (#1 to #2, #2 to #3, and so forth). Only the Rumormonger is told the original rumor directly.
4. The rest of the class observes what happens as the rumor is repeated by one student to the next.

**Discussion:**
- What did you observe?
- How did the original rumor change?
- Which parts of the rumor seemed to change the most throughout the activity?
- Discuss how many times people start rumors about other people who are different from themselves as a result of fear or misunderstanding their differences.
- Introduce person-first language.

**Journal Writing:** Ask students to write about a time when a rumor was spread about them or about someone they know. Ask students to describe how they felt, what they did about the rumor, and perhaps what they could have done differently.

**Role Playing:** Discuss rumors that might be spread in different types of environments (e.g., work environments, sports events, social situations). Present students with scenarios resulting from the rumors, and discuss how to respond appropriately in each case.

Figure 1.   "I heard a rumor" lesson plan. (Work environment sample rumor role-play from Windmills Attitudinal Training Program [Pimentel, 1981].)

*(continued)*

Figure 1.  *(continued)*

**Sample Rumors:**

1. *Disability issues*—I was walking through the front office this morning when I heard the vice-principal talking with one of the counselors. They were talking about some new students with disabilities who are going to be attending this school next fall. I don't know where they're coming from, but it sounded like some of them can't walk or talk or even go to the bathroom by themselves. I heard that we were all going to get them in our classes, but I don't know whether the teachers will get extra help. I don't know what we'll do with them; we have enough kids in our classes as it is.

2. *School change issues* (e.g., block schedules)—I heard a couple of my teachers talking about the new block schedule that the whole staff is going to vote on next week. One was saying that she was excited because she can do more activities in the class instead of feeling as if she has to cover the material in such a short amount of time. The other was saying that she was OK with it but that she was afraid that some of the other teachers would end up lecturing the kids for twice as long as they do now. If they don't learn how to teach us differently, can you imagine how long these class periods are going to seem? It's bad enough just trying to stay awake for 54 minutes!

3. *Work environment role-play*—I was walking through the administrative wing of the building this morning when I heard our manager talking to two human resources executives. They were talking about hiring a person with disabilities to work in our department. I hope they don't fire anyone to make room for a new person. I don't know whether the person is blind or deaf or in a wheelchair, but I heard that they are going to redistribute our workloads. All I can say is that the new person had better carry his or her own weight, or I'm going to the union. They work us hard enough around here as it is.

take place as the rumor is told to each new person. The first student returns and is read the original rumor. When the second student is called, the first student must retell the rumor as he or she remembers it. Each of the other students waiting outside return one at a time, listening and then retelling the latest version of the rumor. After all of the students are in the room, the last student is given the original rumor to read aloud. The class then discusses the changes that they observed, and students share similar experiences that they may have had with rumors. In this case, the rumor is related to the events of the Holocaust, but the rumor could be about new students with disabilities enrolling in the school, the institution of a new school schedule, or changing requirements for grades and portfolios.

## English

Ms. Pratt, a special educator, teamed with the sophomore English teacher during the *Romeo and Juliet* unit. They coordinated a number of activities that generated discussion of names, labels, stereotypes, assumptions, relationships to gang situations, and more. One of the activities that the students especially liked was the day on which every student was labeled. Ms. Pratt prepared labels including *homeless person, politician, person who is blind, cheerleader, person with HIV/AIDS, university professor, new immigrant who speaks no English,* and so forth, and placed them on students' backs. Students could not see their own labels and were directed to walk around as if they were at a social function. Students addressed their classmates as if they were talking to a person with that particular characteristic or identity, without divulging the other student's exact label. Each student had to guess his or her own label based on the conversation that others initiated. The students readily joined in the role-play, building on their prior knowledge and experience. The debriefing brought up many questions about the assumptions that students had about others based on labels. Of course, the conversation then returned to how the Montagues and Capulets did the same thing and how stereotypes and prejudice are all too easily perpetuated. Such activities serve as a vehicle for teaching disability-related information without focusing exclusively on the subject of disability. (See Figure 2 for a stereotype label lesson plan, and see Table 4 for a list of suggested literature with disability themes.)

## Tech Core

Building on his relationship with Mr. Alexander from Tech Core (a rotation through technical classes including electronics, engineering, and design), Mr. Rivino offered to team teach during several of the sophomore and junior classes. Mr. Rivino introduced the use of assistive technology within the context of the class, which is typically conducted through learning stations completed by one or two students at a time. Here is how he started the class. Ten numbered assistive technology devices were set up around the room. Some were commercially available items, some were modified or customized devices, and others were generic items that were used in different ways by people with disabilities. The students were asked to walk

## Stereotype Labels Lesson Plan

**Overview:** We all assume a great deal about each other, particularly when we use labels as a main source of information. It is easy to say that we are open to meeting new people and that we do not prejudge others based on their appearance or status, but it is more difficult to actually and honestly accomplish that. The following classroom activity helps to bring some unacknowledged biases out into the open.

### Objectives:
- To recognize that stereotypes can be damaging
- To recognize individual bias and prejudice that may not be obvious
- To learn positive and nonconfrontational strategies to change prejudicial thinking based on stereotypes

### Materials/Preparation:
- Construction paper, pins, and self-adhesive address labels printed with words that describe social roles or types of people (e.g., homeless person, person who uses a wheelchair, politician, person with human immunodeficiency virus [HIV], person who is blind, football cheerleader, professional basketball player, rock singer, movie star, high school teacher, police officer, homemaker, accountant). Prepare enough labels so that there is one for each student in the classroom.
- Attach one label to the back of each student so that the student cannot see his or her own label.

### Activity:
Set the scene. The students are to mingle as if they were at a community event that is open to the public. Students are to address their classmates as if they were talking to a person with that particular characteristic or identity without divulging their classmates' exact label. Each student gathers clues about his or her own identity and will eventually attempt to guess his or her label based on conversations that other students have initiated with him or her.

### Discussion:
- After determining that most students are ready to guess their identities, instruct all students to arrange their chairs in a circle. Ask students to announce their identities one-by-one, and then check their labels for accuracy. Ask students to share examples of what their classmates said to them and how they made the connection between what was said to them and their label.
- Were the stereotypes accurate? Can exceptions to the stereotypes be given? How are these stereotypes perpetuated in society?

Figure 2.   Stereotype labels lesson plan.

Table 4.    Resource list: Literature with disability themes

### English

Baldwin, J. (1972). *No name in the street.* New York: Doubleday.

Hurst, J. (1996). The scarlet ibis: A classic story of brotherhood. In *Prentice-Hall literature gold* (4th ed., pp. 181–190). Upper Saddle River, NJ: Prentice-Hall.

Saxton, M., & Howe, F. (Eds.). (1987). *An anthology of literature by and about women with disabilities.* New York: Feminist Press of the City University of New York.

Steinbeck, J. (1938). *Of mice and men.* New York: The Modern Library.

Tyler, A. (1996). Average waves in unprotected waters. In *Prentice-Hall literature: The American experience* (4th ed., pp. 872–878). Upper Saddle River, NJ: Prentice-Hall.

### History

Eisenberg, M., Griggins, C., & Duval, R. (Eds.). (1982). *Disabled people as second-class citizens.* New York: Springer.

Fine, M., & Asch, A. (Eds.). (1988). *Women with disabilities: Essays in psychology, culture, and politics.* Philadelphia: Temple University Press.

Friedlander, H. (1995). *The origins of Nazi genocide: From euthanasia to the final solution.* Chapel Hill: University of North Carolina Press.

Gallagher, H. (1985). *FDR's splendid deception.* New York: Dodd Mead.

Percy, S. (1989). *Disability, civil rights, and public policy.* Birmingham: University of Alabama Press.

Shapiro, J. (1993). *No pity: People with disabilities forging a new civil rights movement.* New York: Times Books.

### Disability Literature

Hevey, D. (1992). *The creatures time forgot: Photography and disability imagery.* London: Routledge.

Hockenberry, J. (1995). *Moving violations: War zones, wheelchairs, and declarations of independence.* New York: Hyperion.

Lane, H. (1984). *When the mind hears: A history of the deaf.* New York: Random House.

### On-Line Resources

Classroom Connect: http://www.classroom.net/

Literature Resources for the High School and College Student: http://www.teleport.com/~mgroves/

The Complete Works of William Shakespeare: http://the-tech.mit.edu//Shakespeare/

Responses to the Holocaust: http://jefferson.village.virginia.edu/holocaust/response.html

The WWW Virtual Library: http://www.w3.org/hypertext/DataSources/bySubject/Overview.html

---

around and look at each device and write down its name and/or function. When they were finished, Mr. Rivino held up each device, asked for the students' ideas, and then provided the correct answers. Questions about universal and ergonomic design, job accommodations, and environmental controls were discussed, followed by slides and videotape clips of people with disabilities using assistive technology in a variety of environments. Some of the students were interested in working on adaptations for peers with disabilities, including a few who wanted to incorporate these ideas into their entries for the county's Inventors' Showcase.

## Advisory Period

Many high schools include an advisory period, which may be a homeroom meeting at the beginning of the day when announcements are made. Other schools use this time to discuss personal and social issues and to plan community service activities. When the latter is the purpose of the class, students are typically grouped to include many age levels so that discussions about relationships with one another and with their communities take on new dimensions. One of the activities used in this context is "Orange is More than a Color" (see Figure 3). Each student is given an orange for a few minutes and instructed to bond with it.

> Smell it, look at it, touch it, really get to know your orange. Okay, do you know your orange now? Good, because after I gather them all in this box, you're going to find your own orange again. [Everyone puts their orange in the box, and students then form a large circle around the room.] I'm going to pass each orange, one at a time, to the person on my right. Look at the orange; if it's not yours, keep passing it to the right. When you find your orange, keep it and just keep passing the others as they make their way around the circle. Did everyone find their own orange? [*If not, some negotiation may be required!*] What are some characteristics shared by all of the oranges? How did you find your orange? What was unique about it? As you open it, is there anything unique on the inside that you might not have seen? Like your orange, what special characteristics, qualities, and hidden talents do you each have? Turn to the person next to you and share some ideas. [*After students share in pairs, discuss in the whole group.*]

Students participating in this type of activity (see Figures 3 and 4 for lesson plans) are remarkably open about their unique features. Often discussions of hidden talents can lead to questions or statements about hidden disabilities. Students typically have questions about how people cope with their disabilities or whether it is true that people develop extraordinary talents to compensate for their

---

**"Orange is More than a Color" Lesson Plan**

**Overview:** Although many of us can be described as having many features and characteristics in common, each of us has unique qualities and talents. Identifying uniqueness as a resource rather than as a liability is the goal of this activity.

**Objectives:**
- To identify unique talents and build self-esteem
- To encourage discussion and acceptance of individual differences
- To educate students about inclusive schooling

**Materials/Preparation:**
- One orange for each student and one box or basket to collect all of the oranges
- Chart paper and pens
- Hang up chart paper with topics already written on it (e.g., "How am I unique?" "We all have things in common").

**Activity:**
1. Hand out one orange to each student, and ask students to "get to know" their orange.
2. Collect all of the oranges in a box, and let students know that they are going to find their oranges again as the box is passed around the circle.
3. Begin passing the oranges around the circle, and direct students to keep the one that they believe to be their own orange and pass the rest to the next student in the circle. Have them continue until everyone believes that they have their original orange.

**Discussion:**
- How did you identify your orange?
- How do you think this activity relates to people?
- How are you unique? (List ideas on chart paper entitled "How am I unique?")
- Discuss what all of the students in the class have in common. (List these on chart paper entitled "We all have things in common.")
- Identify talents and/or resources that might be useful to each other. Make a master list, and give a copy of it to each student.

---

Figure 3.   "Orange is more than a color" lesson plan.

disabilities. Discussing stereotypes, assumptions, and myths provides food for thought over a number of class meetings. Some teachers follow up with related activities. Students in one of the senior advisory classes made a list of their skills, connections, or other talents that they might provide to one another as resources. Another teacher assigned the class to keep a journal of remarks that they overheard about people with disabilities. Students in this class began to pay more attention to the language that was used in their school, social, and work environments. Many were shocked at the level of rudeness and disrespect that they overheard, not only from their peers but also, unfortunately, from adults in their lives. The next step was to decide how they were going to take action to make a difference. Although they knew how they should react, students found it very difficult actually to confront friends without embarrassing or belittling them. Opening the dialogue helped the students to figure out what to do the next time they heard an offensive remark. Role-playing a number of scenarios gave them confidence and provided opportunities for practice and feedback in a safe environment.

## CONCLUSIONS

The following excerpt is taken from one student's journal:

> Before I began my senior year, my thoughts and perceptions were totally different from what they are now. Before I only felt pity and embarrassment for people with, or as I thought suffering from, disabilities. But through classes, group examples, lectures and guest speakers, I can't stress enough how much I have learned!
>
> I realized that people with disabilities experience everything I do. Desires, dreams, hopes, goals—nothing is different, and most important, it's not a punishment! Yet it seems, before, I often punished those who are different by not accepting them for who they are. Not to make excuses, but I feel some of this is rooted in my past ignorance and fear that society has created.
>
> People with disabilities should not be cast in a shadow of doubt; rather, they should be accepted by all as human beings. Their courage and outlook on life should be enough to open our eyes to the truth, and my eyes have been opened because of these new experiences. I will continue to do my best to reveal and pass it on to others who were just as ignorant as I was.

Change depends on involving individuals at all levels of the school organization: students, teachers, administrators, and community partners (families, businesses, and universities). For example,

### "Life is Like a Box of Chocolates" Lesson Plan

**Overview:** Just like the old saying, "You can't judge a book by its cover," you can't always tell what a person is like on the inside without taking the time to get better acquainted. This activity is a fun way to open this discussion.

**Objectives:**

- To encourage students not to make judgments about a person without really knowing them
- To promote respect for diversity

**Materials/Preparation:**

- Chocolate candies whose soft centers are not easily identified. Buy enough chocolates so that each student in the class gets one.
- Assign students to groups of 8-10 students, and identify a recorder for each group. The recorder will need paper and a pencil.

**Activity:**

1. Place chocolates in a box or on a tray for each group. Each student chooses a chocolate, but students are asked not to eat their chocolates yet.
2. One at a time, students are asked to predict the type of filling that is in their chocolates and then take a bite of their candies. The recorder keeps track of correct and incorrect guesses, adding up the totals at the end of the activity. Each recorder writes on the chalkboard or overhead projector the totals from his or her group.

**Discussion:**

- How many correct and how many incorrect guesses are there? What percentages of right and wrong answers are there?
- What have you learned from this activity? How can this lesson be applied to people? (You can't tell what people are like by judging them only on what you can see. It's important to get to know what people are like on the inside.)
- What are some of the talents and abilities that you have that people may not notice just by looking at you?
- How often do you think certain things about a person because the person has a disability, is of the opposite sex, or has a different skin color from you when in fact you don't really know that person? Can you describe situations in which this has occurred in your own experience?
- What were some of the reactions that you have had to a person you've met who is different from you? Did those opinions change once you got to know that person?

Figure 4.    "Life is like a box of chocolates" lesson plan.

at the classroom level, teachers provide students with daily opportunities to recognize the value in one another. Lessons about diversity and unique qualities are infused into core literature, cooperative learning activities, and experiential learning opportunities. At the building level, administrators take responsibility for setting the tone for acceptance and inclusive practices for all students, regardless of labels. Administrators may also need to reevaluate allocation of resources and staff development training strategies. At the community level, partnerships are developed with neighborhood businesses, civic organizations, and other local resources to demonstrate and encourage collaboration. Leadership may be demonstrated by any stakeholder during the process of school change. At Adams High School, changes have occurred and continue to take place at all of these levels. Gaining a new perspective on a regular basis is essential because change is a process, not an event.

# 7

# "A Community of Learners Born of Trust, Respect, and Courage"

## The Foundation of Inclusion and School Reform at Jefferson High School

Cheryl M. Jorgensen

A lot has been written about you seniors, particularly, it seems, in the last week, and about your exploits over the past 4 years. I think the bottom line, though, is that you have established a set of standards for future classes that will be very tough to match. I must tell all of you and your parents and your friends and your relatives here today that you are the most awesome class I have known in my 22 years as a school administrator. I think we all know that sitting in front of us today are some of the most powerful scholars, athletes, artists, dramatists, singers, and some of the most creative talents in the state and in this country. And sitting in front of us are people who also contributed 10,000 hours or more of community service. This is a very special group, and I'm tremendously proud of them.

With these words, Robert Mackin, principal of Jefferson High School, convened the 1996 graduation exercises for the first class of students to progress through all 4 years at Jefferson High School (Jorgensen, Mroczka, & Williams, 1999). Although all principals express pride in their graduates, this class truly was special. The students not only were accomplished academically and active in a wide variety of extracurricular pursuits but also were living proof of the positive impact of two complementary educational innovations—the school reform principles espoused by the Coalition of Essential Schools and the inclusive education movement (Sizer, 1989; Villa, Thousand, Stainback, & Stainback, 1992). Although numerous high schools throughout the United States are engaged in a variety of general education reforms and perhaps a smaller number practice inclusion, few are committed to implementing both reforms simultaneously.

This chapter describes the principles and practices that characterize this break-the-mold school and concludes with a discussion of some of the challenges that will undoubtedly be faced by other schools engaged in similar reform efforts. Through examples and reflective comments of students, parents, teachers, and administrators, the chapter attempts to answer the question, "How can schools be restructured so that the inclusion of every student in the mainstream of general education is a necessary condition for the achievement of excellence by all?"

## HISTORY AND BACKGROUND

Jefferson High School is located in a rural community in a racially homogeneous part of New England. Although some families in the area experience economic hardship, the community is by and large affluent. Despite the cultural homogeneity of the community, people's political views run the gamut from liberal to libertarian to conservative. Parents of every political persuasion are passionate about local education issues and participate actively in school and town governance.

Because of a growing student population in the nearby regional high school in the late 1980s and the community's concern about a lack of control over the education of students who attended that school, a significant majority of the citizenry supported a proposal for a new high school. Several years of planning preceded ground breaking, with a large number of people serving on committees that discussed every aspect of the new school, including location, architecture, landscaping, philosophy, governance, and curriculum. The leadership of superintendent Richard Lalley was key to the emerging philosophy of respect and value for all students (Jorgensen et al., 1999), who stated the following:

> How do you create an environment where all children can excel—all children, not some children or most of the children, but all of the children? Every child is so important, so unique, that to do anything less is a travesty. It's a simple view, not complicated. It's nice that the research supports it. But even if the research didn't support it, I wouldn't care, because essentially schools need to be places where every child is respected for what he or she can do and worked with to raise that child's level of performance as high as we possibly can before we let them out into the cruel world where they're not going to have our support. They're going to have to fend for themselves, so let's give them the skills [they'll need], and I think more importantly than anything, the belief in themselves, that they can be successful. If we do that, I go home happy. (Jorgensen et al., 1999)

After an extensive reading of education literature, visiting other high schools, and hosting presentations by university faculty and proponents of several different school reform theories, the school board decided to adopt the principles of the Coalition of Essential Schools, which was founded by Theodore Sizer at Brown University (Sizer, 1989). An administrative planning team, including the newly recruited Principal Mackin, worked together the year prior to Jefferson's opening to hone the school's mission statement, hire faculty, and begin to operationalize the Coalition's principles into the daily workings of a 550-student high school, which are described in detail throughout the remainder of this chapter.

## PHILOSOPHICAL PRINCIPLES

A variety of philosophical and pedagogical beliefs provide guideposts for the myriad of decisions that are made every day at Jefferson High School. The relationships among these beliefs and the issues of school reform and inclusion are discussed in the following sections.

### Mission Statement

> The mission statement. [*Pause*] The mission statement. We've got a mission statement. Freshman year, we have to read the mission statement. Dissect it and break it apart. As a community we aspire to learn and respect our school. Don't lie and cheat. Be a good kid. That's the gist of it. I don't memorize it, but I know what it's about. (Jorgensen et al., 1999)

Although the tenth-grade student just quoted has missed important details of the Jefferson mission statement, the fact that he knows that it exists, can name some of the general principles it contains, and remembers the attention it was given during his ninth-grade year illustrates that Jefferson's most important guiding principle is not just a collection of fancy words relegated to the back of the district's annual report. Here is the Jefferson High School mission statement in its entirety:

> Jefferson High School aspires to be a community of learners born of respect, trust, and courage. We consciously commit ourselves
>
> To support and engage an individual's unique gifts, passions, and intentions
>
> To develop and empower the mind, body, and heart
>
> To challenge and expand the comfortable limits of thought, tolerance, and performance
>
> To inspire and honor the active stewardship of family, nation, and globe

Line by line, the mission statement illustrates respect for and celebration of diversity:

- "A community of learners" implies that learning must be communal and collaborative and that segregation of students is antithetical to the values of a community.
- "To support and engage an individual's unique gifts, passions,

and intentions" acknowledges that all students are different; it is the school's responsibility to get to know every student and then offer learning opportunities that tap into all students' talents, interests, and goals and to provide support when they falter.

- "To develop and empower the mind, body, and heart" lays to rest the notion that a school's only mission is intellectual. This declaration puts schools in partnership with families and other community agencies to educate students' minds, help them attain physical well-being, and develop their character and citizenship.

- "To challenge and expand the comfortable limits of thought, tolerance, and performance" signals that Jefferson will make the education process uncomfortable at times. Jefferson helps students develop a healthy intellectual curiosity and cynicism not only toward matters of hard science but also toward issues such as civil rights; personal freedom, order, and responsibility; the role of government in the lives of ordinary citizens; ethical issues regarding biotechnology; and so forth.

- "To inspire and honor the active stewardship of family, nation, and globe" is a statement in which Jefferson recognizes that the ultimate goal of education is to prepare students to be responsible citizens in a democracy, evidenced by responsible family life, service to the community, and stewardship of the earth's natural resources.

Although the mission statement is engraved on the wall in Jefferson's main lobby, it is also a living, breathing document that guides individual action and schoolwide policy decisions. It is not uncommon to overhear a group of teachers engaged in some curricular or administrative discussion asking themselves, "How will this exhibition that we are planning for students tap into each student's passions and interests?" and, "As we develop our discipline policy, how will we guide our students to become not only rule followers but also responsible citizens here in the building and in the community?"

## Jefferson Six

Although the mission statement expresses the overarching philosophy of the school, the Jefferson Six (*Rules of the Road*, n.d.), a formal code of conduct for students, speaks directly to the behavior that is expected of students within this unusual climate of respect, trust, and freedom:

1. Respect and encourage the right to teach and the right to learn at all times.
2. Be actively engaged in the learning process; ask questions, collaborate, and seek solutions.
3. Be on time to fulfill your daily commitments.
4. Be appropriate; demonstrate behavior that is considerate of the community, the campus, and yourself.
5. Be truthful; communicate honestly.
6. Be responsible and accountable for your choices.

From the time they begin the ninth grade until the time they graduate, students are educated about the Jefferson Six within many environments and by a variety of school personnel, including within their advisory groups; in social studies classes, in which broader historical and social issues are discussed that touch on issues of individual freedom and community responsibility; during assemblies; at community council and class meetings; and, should the need arise, as a part of disciplinary proceedings with guidance counselors or peer conduct boards. When students misbehave, the Jefferson Six become the framework through which teachers guide students to examine the impact of their behavior on the community, rather than simply focus on an infraction of the rules.

## Common Principles of the Coalition of Essential Schools

As a member of the Coalition of Essential Schools, Jefferson uses the Coalition's common principles to guide decisions about curriculum, instruction, and assessment; to define the relationships among teachers, students, administrators, and the community; and to support the need for organizational structures that enable teachers to work collaboratively (Sizer, 1989). Although there were nine Coalition principles when Jefferson first opened, a tenth has been added that mirrors Jefferson's commitment to equity and excellence. The 10 common principles of the Coalition of Essential Schools are as follows:

1. Focus on helping students use their minds well.
2. Set a few simple but clear goals. "Less is more" regarding coverage of the curriculum.

3. The school's goals should apply to all students, although the means of working toward these goals will vary as do the students themselves.

4. Teaching and learning should be personalized.

5. The governing metaphors of the school should be "student as worker" and "teacher as coach" rather than "student as passive learner" and "teacher as deliverer of instructional services."

6. Diplomas should be awarded upon a successful demonstration of mastery through performance-based exhibitions.

7. The tone of the school should stress unanxious expectation.

8. The principal and teachers should perceive themselves as generalists first and specialists second.

9. Teachers should have substantial time for collective planning, they should be responsible for no more than 80 students, and the overall school budget should not be more than 10% higher than that of a traditional high school.

10. The school should demonstrate nondiscriminatory and inclusive policies, practices, and pedagogies. It should model democratic practices that involve all who are directly affected by the school. The school should honor diversity and build on the strengths of its communities, deliberately and explicitly challenging all forms of inequity.

In a community like Jefferson's, many families are financially able to send their sons or daughters to private schools. One parent who considered this option but chose Jefferson instead commented on the "Jefferson difference" with regard to the intellectual growth of her son, who had been labeled as one of those "in the middle, solid B students." She said,

> We had considered private school options. Brian is a good plugger, is very self-motivated when he has set goals. He did very well in middle school when he had a textbook and a chapter that he had to know and be tested on. And then he came here, and he really felt lost and was uncomfortable without that security blanket of the textbook. So about the middle of the year, [his dad and I] met with his teachers, and we really asked them, did they think that this was the right environment for a student like Brian, who wasn't going to do any extra reading on his own? So we really went around and around and investigated other schools and kept in close contact with his teachers, and then a series of things happened. [Brian's] sister came home with a social studies test, and she was to memorize the countries of Europe and their capi-

tals. Brian looked over and said, "What are you wasting your time
doing that for?" And she said, "Well, it's my assignment. We're going
to have a blank map, and we have to identify the countries and capi-
tals." So he came and looked at it and said, "First of all, that map is out
of date. Some of those countries don't even exist any more. You know,
if you know how to find the information, why would you waste your
time memorizing?" So that really turned on a light bulb in our minds.
He had made a huge leap to a higher level of thinking, and he didn't
realize that.

## Inclusion Philosophy

Jefferson High School is a school of inclusion. It is our strong belief
that all students can learn and that as much as possible, all students
should be given the opportunity to stretch themselves academically
across the school's curriculum. Mixed ability grouping is utilized in
most classroom settings. This means that students who have historically been tracked into lower level courses and students "coded" with
learning disabilities are also asked to meet high standards, but are
given additional time and the support of a teacher when necessary.
(Jorgensen et al., 1999)

Does a truly inclusive school need an inclusion philosophy? In
an ideal world, it probably would not. Given the daily challenges of
maintaining the commitment to inclusive practices, however, a public acknowledgment of beliefs can serve to buoy teachers and administrators when the going gets tough.

Mike Reddington, a 1996 graduate who went on to major in
special education in college, expressed his views about the inclusion
of a friend and classmate:

I think it's awesome that [he] was fully included, especially because he
gets to be with us. . . . He's not walking down a different hallway
wondering what it's like to be us; he's right with us. He's doing the
same things we're doing. He played on the football team with us; I
worked with him in a regular outside-of-school job, and I think the
school leads to that because he feels comfortable with us. He's getting
the same education we are and he feels like one of us . . . like one of
the guys; he is one of the guys. (Jorgensen et al., 1999)

The mother of another student expressed amazement that her
son, Rob, had developed a deeper understanding of people with disabilities, despite the fact that he had never known any students with
significant disabilities prior to coming to Jefferson. She said,

He said that [the speech they gave at the inclusion conference] the audience cry. I think he was kind of happy about that. He really enjoyed meeting the other kids that are involved [in youth leadership activities around inclusion]. There's something; they really clicked. Not only the kids helping the special needs kids but he loved meeting the other special needs kids. I love his words when he describes them because he'll come home and tell me about this girl named Julie and [say,] "She's so cute, mom. She did that and did this and this person you wouldn't believe what they can do" and on and on. And then you see pictures of these children, and cute is not the word that I would have chosen. That's what he sees. He sees something different. He sees the soul or something. Which is a gift. Which is something I'm glad he's found. (Jorgensen et al., 1999)

## Cultural Indicators

In a keynote address at the 1997 Equity and Excellence Conference, Principal Mackin of Jefferson High School drew sharp contrasts between several cultural indicators of inclusive, reform-minded schools and schools in which students are tracked or segregated in special education classes (Mackin, 1997). These differences in cultural indicators are summarized in Table 1 (Jorgensen, 1998).

Of course, for most students, their analysis of the Jefferson climate is much more down to earth. A ninth grader expressed students' feelings in the teen slang of her generation:

Table 1.   Differences between an inclusive, restructuring high school and a traditional high school

| Inclusive, restructuring high school | Traditional high school |
| --- | --- |
| Innovation and risk taking | Status quo and safe compliance |
| Inquiring | Accepting |
| Trust | Suspicion |
| Coaching | Telling |
| Active learning | Passive learning |
| Heterogeneity | Homogeneity |
| Personalized education | Assembly-line education |
| Exhibitions of performance | Tests of memory |
| Global consciousness | Self-centeredness |
| Holistic, interdisciplinary learning | Subject-focused learning |
| High expectations for all | Challenge for only the elite |
| Empowerment | Subservience |
| Flexibility | Rigidity |
| Democracy and justice | Authoritarian control |

.   It's so much more freedom, and so much more, like, teachers are almost your friends; you get a lot more respect in some ways. I don't
know. It's really different from a lot of the other high schools, because,
like, the teachers don't lecture you, but they talk with you. You have
discussions instead of being talked at, which, like, keeps my attention. (Jorgensen et al., 1999)

Mackin further outlined six interconnected variables that hold
together all of Jefferson's various philosophical beliefs. The first variable is a mind-set—a multidimensional set of beliefs including a deeply
felt conviction that all students can learn to use their minds well,
that each and every student must be known well by at least one
adult in the school, and that students must have a stake in Jefferson's
success. The second element that gives strength to the entire fabric
of Jefferson's culture is the mission statement to which all of the
school's employees subscribe. The third essential element is the commitment by teachers and administrators to continual renewal of the
school's deepest values by a conscious focus on the mission and its
relationship to daily practice. The fourth variable associated with
Jefferson's success is the notion that, within an environment of trust
and respect, most students will live up to high expectations for moral
and ethical behavior. Fifth, Jefferson is a democratic society in which
students are asked to voice their ideas and beliefs in preparation for
their participation as responsible citizens in their communities. The
last element, when all of these pieces are in place, is that Jefferson
believes that new, higher norms of achievement will result—that the
creation of an inclusive, democratic school culture and climate is
good for the development of not only students' character but also
their intellects.

The work of Norman Kunc (1992) linking belonging and learning supports Jefferson's beliefs that optimal learning cannot occur
unless students have a sense of belonging. Although some people
manage to perform well enough when they are segregated or
marginalized, they will inevitably do better when they believe that
they are valued and part of an inclusive community of learners.

## PRACTICES

Philosophical statements have little meaning unless they are trans-
lated into daily practice in the classroom. The Jefferson practices

that seem most closely related to the successful inclusion and achievement of students with disabilities are briefly described after an overview of Jefferson's student enrollment and grade structure. An expanded discussion of learning standards and the curriculum design process is presented in recognition of their importance in the daily lives of Jefferson's teachers and students.

## Student Enrollment and Grade Structure

Although the school opened with approximately 550 students, it has grown steadily and as of 1999 houses 850 students. The ninth and tenth grades each comprise two large teams and one miniteam of students and teachers. Each large team has approximately 90 students, and 30 students are assigned to each miniteam. Teams are staffed by English, social studies, science, math, and special education teachers or by aides. (For a sample block schedule for ninth- and tenth-graders, see p. 126; the roles and responsibilities of the Jefferson learning specialist are described later in this chapter.) The eleventh and twelfth grades are organized much like a traditional high school, with seven periods in a day. Two periods are blocked together in these upper-division grades so that teachers can work collaboratively to teach interdisciplinary junior and senior seminar classes addressing English and history.

## Advisory Groups

Every day groups of about 10 students meet for 30 minutes with a staff member (faculty, administrators, teaching assistants, custodial staff) for an advisory period. Advisory period is a time for students to talk about academic, social, school, and world issues; discuss issues related to the school's discipline policy; plan and carry out community service projects; receive instruction in study and organizational skills; and engage in career exploration and graduation-planning activities. The close, personal nature of the relationship between the advisor and his or her students helps prevent problems with truancy, academic failure, and substance abuse and serves as a conduit for home–school communication. Students with disabilities benefit from this system because more people are looking out for them than just their special education service coordinator.

## Heterogeneous Grouping and Inclusion

Principal Mackin of Jefferson High described the community concerns related to its heterogeneous grouping and inclusion philosophies as follows:

> When we first opened here at Jefferson High School, we were deeply committed to inclusion [and heterogeneous grouping]. The community concerns . . . always seem to derive from the parents of the "most able" kids, the prospective honors kids. And I've heard this for 20 years as I've attempted to untrack schools everywhere that I've been. I believe, and I think our staff believes, very strongly that tracking is wrong, and that heterogeneous grouping can work to the benefit of all kids. The bottom line is you want to shoot for high standards for all kids, insist that they make it, insist that support is provided by the school, by the teacher within the classroom. . . .
>
> I think what's happened over the past 5 years is that the commitment has remained steadfast, but we've become more realistic about how difficult it is for teachers to ensure that heterogeneity works in every classroom. So what we found is that through lots of staff development efforts, we've tried to get teachers up to speed, so that in fact they would challenge all kids. The real trick to heterogeneous grouping is to ensure that you can challenge a whole range of kids in every classroom. And that's hard work for teachers. For teachers to acquire those skills, they need to work on it, and working . . . collaboratively is the way we've found that it's best. And if we can get some good resources in to help support teachers, then it ultimately can be effective and can work for everybody. (Jorgensen et al., 1999)

All students with disabilities at Jefferson (who compose approximately 15% of the total student population at Jefferson) are enrolled in nontracked, heterogeneous general education classes. There are no classes, programs, or rooms for students with disabilities, and, likewise, all classes and extracurricular activities are open to all students. In the ninth and tenth grades, all students enroll in the same English, social studies, science, and math classes. There are no remedial, general, college prep, or honors courses. Within each major unit of study in all courses, any student can elect to do the honors challenge arranged by contract between the student and the teacher. Successful completion of honors work results in a special designation on the report card and a corresponding boost in the student's grade-point average for class-rank purposes.

In the eleventh and twelfth grades, students are grouped heterogeneously in most English, social studies, science, math, language, and technology classes, although some homogeneity exists in some upper-level courses. Students with disabilities nevertheless are enrolled in classes at all course levels.

The decision not to track and to group students heterogeneously was made during the year of planning prior to Jefferson's opening, and it continues to be one of the more controversial issues for the community. Concerns raised by parents or community members reflect a number of myths and commonly held beliefs about ability grouping, including the following:

- Ability grouping promotes achievement within all tracks because students can learn at their own rate with students who are similar to them.
- Teachers can tailor instruction better when their students are homogeneous with respect to ability, learning styles, and rate of learning.
- Less capable students will get lost and their self-esteem will suffer if they are in heterogeneous classes.
- More able students will be held back by being in heterogeneous classes.
- It is easier for teachers to teach homogeneous classes.
- It is easy to determine which track or group a student ought to be in.
- If tracking and ability grouping are eliminated, the curriculum as a whole will be watered down because teachers will lower their expectations (i.e., the curriculum standards) and slow the pace of instruction to reach the most challenged learners in the classroom. (Jorgensen, Fisher, Sax, & Skoglund, 1998, p. 63)

Ability grouping and tracking have negative social and academic consequences for students with disabilities. The existence of separate special education classes is actually legitimized by tracking in general education. Even when students with disabilities are placed in general education classes within a traditionally tracked curriculum, they cluster in the lower-track classes that have a less challenging curriculum, more students with behavior problems, and sometimes less qualified and less respected teachers (Jorgensen et al., 1998).

Findings from the research on tracking are summarized in Table 2. The research indicates that ability grouping does not result in higher academic achievement for the majority of students, often leads to

116     Jorgensen

Table 2.   Summary of research on tracking and ability grouping

| Research finding | Sources |
| --- | --- |
| There is little evidence that ability grouping or tracking improves academic achievement, although overwhelming evidence shows that tracking retards the academic progress of students in low- and middle-ability groupings. A few studies have found that tracking the highest-achieving students increases their academic performance. | Cotton and Savard (1981) Featherstone (1987) Kulik and Kulik (1982) Oakes (1985) Rowan and Miracle (1983) Slavin (1987) |
| Expectations of students are higher and instructional practices more effective in higher-track classes. | Good and Brophy (1987) Oakes (1985) Rist (1970) |
| Ability grouping and tracking widens the achievement and knowledge gap between students. | Rist (1970) Weisendanger and Birlen (1981) |
| Ability grouping reduces expectations for students' future educational aspirations beyond high school. | Rosenbaum (1976) Schaefer and Olexa (1971) |
| Low-ability grouped students, including those in special education classes, have lower self-esteem and expectations as well as the social stigma of being less smart. | George (1988) Vanfossen, Jones, and Spade (1987) |
| Ability grouping and tracking have negative effects on students' relationships. | Sorenson and Hallinan (1986) |

stigmatization of students in lower tracks, and has a negative impact on students' self-esteem and postgraduation plans (Jorgensen et al., 1998).

During the 1995 school year, a group of concerned parents and citizens obtained enough community support to bring up the issue of heterogeneous grouping for a vote at the annual town meeting, which is the form of local government in many New England communities. In the weeks prior to the meeting, several special school board meetings were held to invite open public comment on the issue. Groups of teachers, students, administrators, and parents spoke for and against heterogeneous grouping. In the final analysis, the question was defeated by a margin of 3 to 1 in favor of maintaining Jefferson's heterogeneous grouping practices. Although some students over the years have expressed a dislike for heterogeneous classes, most echo this junior's comments in their support for Jefferson's nontracking policy:

> I mean, a lot of my friends, they have a lot of trouble with stuff, and we sort of accept the fact that everybody's different and everybody helps each other. The kids help each other, and it's so weird; I don't know how to explain it. I mean, there shouldn't be [segregated] classes. I'm totally against that, like an honors class. I like how we're all integrated [in the same] classes so everybody can help each other.

## NEW ROLES FOR SPECIAL EDUCATORS

Kathryn Skoglund, Director of Special Instructional Services at Jefferson, described how the role of the special education teacher is unique at Jefferson:

> The role of the special education person in a school like Jefferson High School has to be unique from what we are accustomed to in special education. We are not in a position any longer of having a great black dividing line down the middle of the classroom, and the classroom teacher saying, "'These are my kids, and these are your kids. Take them away," and, in fact, then the classroom teacher [rarely] lays eyes on that special ed teacher again. There are some basic criteria we look for in this sort of new special educator. One is a much more extensive knowledge of general curriculum. And it isn't just for the [students with disabilities]. . . . Their techniques need to be applicable to the high-end kids [as well]. So we are looking at a kind of generic support person—inherently different from what we have been asking special ed teachers to do in the past. (Jorgensen et al., 1999)

At Jefferson, the role of the special education teacher has evolved from year to year and reflects not only the philosophy of inclusion but also a primary role for support staff in curriculum planning and instruction in the general education classroom. The job description of the learning specialist is presented in Table 3.

Although the configuration changes slightly from year to year, depending on the student composition within each academic team, the typical special education staffing pattern includes the following: a certified special education teacher or aide as a member of each

Table 3.    Job description of Jefferson High School learning specialist

**I.   Instruction**
  1.  Provide instruction to any student for whom the teaching team
      desires assistance.
  2.  Identify and/or gather appropriate instruction materials.
  3.  Assist in adapting materials and instruction.
  4.  Provide small-group and individual instruction in or out of the
      classroom.
  5.  Teach the whole class.
  6.  Keep informed of and assist in using strategies that promote
      inclusion.
  7.  Supervise special education teaching assistants in the classroom.
  8.  Monitor students' academic work.
  9.  Develop and assist in the implementation of behavior management
      plans.

**II.   Assessment and evaluation**
  1.  Grade students.
  2.  Administer and interpret educational tests as necessary.
  3.  Assist in developing appropriate exhibitions and demonstrations.
  4.  Direct special education referrals through the proper channels.
  5.  Facilitate the prereferral process.

**III.   Communication**
  1.  Attend team planning meetings.
  2.  Communicate regularly with parents of students for whom the
      learning specialist is a service coordinator.
  3.  Attend and facilitate update and problem-solving meetings. Keep all
      teachers (including elective and foreign language teachers, guidance
      counselors, and advisors) informed of students' needs and status.
  4.  Provide support for additional personnel involved in meeting
      students' needs as specified in their individualized education
      programs (IEPs).
  5.  Facilitate the use of specialists from outside agencies.

**IV.   Record keeping**
  1.  Develop and write IEPs with input from teaching teams.
  2.  Keep necessary records (e.g., Annual Statement of Program, referrals,
      minutes of meetings, telephone logs).

ninth- and tenth-grade team, a certified teacher and aide assigned to the eleventh grade and another teacher–aide team assigned to the twelfth grade, a districtwide inclusion facilitator who coordinates supports for students with significant cognitive and physical disabilities, and a social worker who supports students across all four grades. Although the state of New Hampshire still maintains a categorical special education teacher certification system, Jefferson teachers are assigned noncategorically to teams. Jefferson recruits teachers who have high school teaching experience; who have extensive knowledge of the general education curriculum; and who have expertise in teaching students with a variety of learning, behavioral, and emotional challenges.

## ACADEMIC SUPPORT

Academic support for students occurs through the development of inclusive curriculum and cooperative teaching as well as in the Academic Support Center or in classrooms not being used for whole-class instruction. All students are encouraged to use the school's Academic Support Center to receive individualized tutoring from a subject area or special education teacher. The center is staffed all day by both general and special education teachers. Students whose work is incomplete or who have done below C-level work are referred to the center by their classroom teacher, and a plan of support is developed by the center's coordinator. The center is also used by students for small-group meetings, for one-to-one tutoring, for chess club meetings, and as a general hangout by students during their free periods.

## STANDARDS AND CURRICULUM DESIGN

The links among Jefferson's learning standards, the way the curriculum is organized, the unit and lesson design process, and the means of assessing student learning are key to the school's ability to challenge and support all students in inclusive general education programs. These topics are discussed next.

### Learning Standards

Learning standards at Jefferson are derived from a combination of local, state, and national criteria. Every tenth grader in the state is required to take a statewide assessment test in the areas of language arts, math, social studies, and science. Although the state does not dictate learning outcomes, it has established curriculum frameworks to assist local districts that wish to improve students' scores on the tests by aligning their local curriculum with the frameworks on which the assessment tests are based. Using guidelines from such national organizations as the National Council of Teachers of English, the National Council of Teachers of Mathematics, and the recommendations for the science curriculum from Project 2061, Jefferson developed its own learning standards in many subject areas, as well as in general categories such as information user, collaborative worker, and effective communicator.

A glance at Jefferson's curriculum as expressed in course offerings and graduation requirements reveals a rather traditional schema. All ninth and tenth graders are enrolled in English, science, social studies, mathematics, wellness (health and physical education), and arts courses. More than 85% of students take a modern or classical language course and, if their schedule allows, one elective per semester. At the junior and senior levels, some diversity of course offerings is available in the sciences and math, but all students are required to enroll in a core humanities course (blending literature and social studies). The real "Jefferson difference" in the classroom occurs, however, when teachers translate learning outcomes into curriculum units and daily lessons.

## Unit and Lesson Design

Dean of Faculty Allison Rowe acknowledged that a strength of Jefferson's curriculum planning process is its flexibility and focus on empowering students to direct their own learning:

> The curriculum-planning process itself is not a linear process; it implies a constant loop of answering the [following] questions: what [do] you want the kid to know, what [do] you want them to be able to do, what are the questions that should drive that learning, what are the resources that you will need, what are the assessments you need to do? So that you're discovering as you go, and the student is discovering what it is they need to do next. And that's a very messy process. It can look chaotic at times. But if you stick with it, as we have, we find that the students begin to understand themselves as learners, begin to be able to develop their own questions, begin to be able to answer the questions themselves: What should I know? What do I need to do in order to learn this? What kind of help do I need, what kind of support? And [the students] begin to become independent learners, which is what it's really all about. (Jorgensen et al., 1999)

The use of heterogeneous grouping, along with high academic standards, forces the need for a unit and lesson design process that accommodates student differences—differences in skill, in interest, in motivation, and in past experiences. Jefferson anchors its unit design process with an essential question that frames the important topic or question being studied and an exhibition or culminating demonstration of learning that will indicate what students have learned. An adaptation of Onosko and Jorgensen's (1998) eight elements of unit and lesson planning illustrates how Jefferson teachers fill in the details between the essential question and the final exhibition during the unit-planning process. The eight elements are presented here as five steps for unit design and three overarching principles that should guide unit design and instruction.

**Planning Step #1: Develop a Central Unit Issue, Problem Statement, or Question**    Jorgensen described the first planning step as follows:

> Structuring a unit of study around an issue, problem, or essential question creates a framework for the learning experience and provides direction and coherence. . . . When all students in a classroom are focused on addressing a common question, differences in learning styles and ability are less important than the commonality of all students constructing meaning in the content area, albeit in a personalized way. (1998, p. 7)

Tenth-grade social studies teacher Cathy Fisher commented on the need for flexibility in the curriculum design process:

> The reality of the day to day is that ideas happen when you are driving to school, or in the shower; it doesn't happen as we all sit down at tables and say, "Let's plan curriculum." So I think it really involves a great amount of flexibility. When we sit down to talk about work that we are planning for kids, we have adopted a certain protocol for it, which centers around the essential questions that we are going to be using and the exhibitions that we're going to be asking kids to do. And to me, it's imperative that the skills then that we work on are the skills needed for the exhibition. And the content is almost on a need-to-know basis. . . . You work on the skills and content that [students] need to successfully complete the exhibition. (Jorgensen et al., 1999)

Examples of essential questions and problem statements that Jefferson uses include the following:

- Can you be free if you are not treated equally?
- What makes us human?
- What is your sense of place?
- How can you tell if an organism is living?
- The more things change, the more they stay the same.

*Planning Step #2: Design a Culminating Project or Exhibition*    The second stage in unit design involves identifying what students will be asked to do at the end of the unit to show that they can answer the question or respond to the problem statement with mastery. Final exhibitions should reflect local, state, and/or national learning standards; should require a public exhibition or performance; and should test not only discipline-specific knowledge but also intellectual and social habits of mind (Sizer, 1992). Examples of Jefferson exhibitions include completing an IRS Form 1040, building a tabletop Spanish village, researching and testifying at a legislative hearing about a proposed bill, designing a robotic arm for a person with a disability, writing a song, developing a proposal for a small business, and participating in a debate about rain forest preservation or development.

Eavesdropping on a collaborative planning session of a team of Jefferson teachers reveals that teachers usually engage in a brainstorming free for all at this stage of unit design, flowing back and forth between ideas for essential questions and culminating exhibitions. In fact, some units arise first from an idea for a great exhibition and the essential question is written to support that culminating project.

*Planning Step #3: Design a Beginning-of-Unit Grabber or Kick-Off Activity*    The hook, or the activity that engages students in the unit, occurs in the first class period in which the unit is introduced. Everyone recognizes the traditional way that new units are introduced: "Okay, everyone, we are going to begin Chapter 5 in our book. Let's all turn to page 165 and skim the chapter outline." Although high-achieving students who are self-motivated (either by the promise of good grades or by genuine interest) go along with almost any teaching style, students with unique learning needs must be actively engaged in a unit right from the start by sensing their own personal stake in the topic. For a class of tenth graders, a Jefferson social studies teacher recreated conditions on a slave ship to kick off a unit on slavery and the Civil War. Following a 20-minute period in which all students were crowded into a marked-off area of the classroom the same size as one level of a slave ship, students wrote entries in a journal or drew pictures that depicted their reaction to the question, "What does it mean to be free?" A science teacher passed out worm-eaten branches from New England pine trees and asked a student to tell "The Story of the Stick" to kick off a unit on conservation. In each case, students were engaged through many of their senses and learning styles, they were asked to consider a provocative issue from a personal perspective, and they were given a chance to express an opinion about a new or unfamiliar topic with no judgments made about the rightness or wrongness of their responses.

**Planning Step #4: Design Interrelated Daily Lessons**   The fourth stage of the unit design process is daily lesson planning. Although traditional teachers certainly attempt to link their daily lessons to one another, the emphasis is usually on breadth of coverage rather than on depth of understanding because the final evaluation is an equally broad assessment of recall through multiple choice and/or comprehensive essay tests. At Jefferson, with its adherence to Coalition principles, less is more and daily lessons are designed to help students learn the content that they need to know for the final exhibition, not every single fact about the topic at hand. My daughter was required to memorize and repeat four- or five-word explanations of 122 facts (people, dates, places, and events) relating to the Civil War when she studied it in the eighth grade. Yet, when I asked her, "How was Dred Scott instrumental in escalating tensions between the North and the South?" she responded, "We don't have to know that, Mom."

Meaningful daily lessons offer students opportunities to identify various viewpoints of positions regarding the unit's central issue or question; identify key concepts, events, or people relating to the issue under consideration; and identify and answer subquestions that need to be answered first to develop a rich understanding of the complexities of the essential question or issue.

**Planning Step #5: Design Multiple Formal and Informal Assessments to Be Conducted Along the Way**   Everyone remembers the horror of finishing a unit feeling pretty confident that they knew the material and then bombing the final exam. Multiple assessments—ones that do not count toward the final unit grade—ought to be planned to provide students with frequent feedback regarding their growing understanding of the topic. These assessments can occur informally as teachers observe students engaging in class discussions. They often include feedback on homework assignments or miniquizzes. Quick whole-class reviews at the beginning or the end of the period can give teachers valuable insight into who gets it and who is confused. Although the form of feedback can be quantitative (e.g., five of six problems correct) or qualitative (e.g., "Your main ideas are well developed, but you need to present more supporting facts"), students should not be graded as they are learning. A classroom in which students are focused on increasing their understanding finds students unfazed by incorrect answers, whereas a classroom in which grades are the reward finds students who cheat, tear up homework marked with the teacher's red pen, refuse to admit confusion and misunderstanding, and so forth.

***Principles Guiding Unit Design and Instruction***    Although not considered planning steps in and of themselves, three overarching principles for accommodating students' differences ought to guide each step of unit design and instruction:

- Providing richly detailed source material that reflects diverse learning styles (e.g., reading materials at different difficulty levels, books on tape, videotapes, models, demonstrations)
- Varying learning and teaching formats (e.g., cooperative groups, whole-class Socratic dialogues, paired learning, teacher-directed tutorials, labs)
- Encouraging varied modes of expression or demonstrations of learning (e.g., essays, oral presentations, slide shows, cartoons, models, blueprints, debates)

English teacher Peggy Silva described how a creative interdisciplinary exhibition allowed one student's talents to shine through her labeled learning disability:

The task [for this unit] was to familiarize the students with the ideas and the people of the 18th century as [the colonists] began to formulate a government. One way to do it is to rely on classroom notes and hand them a lot of information, have conversation about it, and ask them to give back that information. Instead we chose for the students to appear on a talk show called "Meeting of the Minds" suggested to us by Grant Wiggins at a workshop that [the special education teacher] and I attended last summer. The students could pick from a list of important people in the 18th century, . . . research their characters and then become their characters. They give a 3-minute biography of their character and then have to respond to a modern-day question relating to health care, gun control, freedom of speech, etc. [as their character would respond]. One girl in particular has a real dramatic flair [though] she seldom follows through on any work [and has a learning disability]. The fact that she could become Molly Pitcher and have an accent and wear a costume, and that she had to prepare her character, really consumed her and she did a great job. I know now that if I'm to be effective with her for the rest of the year, I have to find a way of combining the information I need her to know and the ability for her to present it to me in a way that engages her. You need to say, "You can succeed, and I've got to figure out how you can succeed."

*A final note:* Without exception, original unit plans created by teachers at Jefferson are always modified once the unit gets under way. Effective teachers respond to teachable moments, veer from planned lessons when reteaching is necessary, skip ahead in the syllabus when pacing is too slow, and so forth. The best-laid plans are continually revised, whereas the framing question and the final exhibition remain constant.

## INNOVATIVE SCHEDULING

One of the first organizational barriers that impede schools' efforts relative to inclusion and broad-based reform is the daily schedule. Jefferson Superintendent Richard Lalley debunked the excuses offered by some who complain that there is not enough time for teachers to experiment with new ways of teaching all students:

Time can always be [used] as an excuse for not accomplishing reform. One way in which Jefferson and other high schools can be seen as being on the same plane is we have the same time that other high schools have. We're equal there. We have no advantage. It's how we structure the time that can make the difference . . . that can provide the planning time. It's how we have teams of teachers working with teams of students at the ninth and tenth grade level. It's that scheduling method that allows the time to be created. Well, any high school can do the same thing. Within the confines of their day, just as we have within our day, they can "create" time. (Jorgensen et al., 1999)

The traditional high school schedule, typified by the seven-period day in which students go from subject to subject after 50-minute classes, results in fragmented instruction and learning; a lack of common planning time for teachers; and an impersonal, hectic school climate. For students with disabilities, short, fragmented classes can be ineffective learning environments. Students often miss important information when teachers rush to get through their material in a short class period. In 50-minute classes, teachers rarely use cooperative learning structures, and students with disabilities miss out on valuable opportunities for social and academic interaction (Jorgensen et al., 1998).

At Jefferson High School, longer blocks of learning time and a daily common planning period were provided for all ninth- and tenth-grade teachers by instituting a teaming structure within a flexible block schedule as follows:

| | |
|---|---|
| 7:30–10:00 A.M. | Academic block |
| 10:00–11:30 A.M. | Electives ("core" teachers have planning time) |
| 11:30 A.M.–12:00 P.M. | Lunch |
| 12:00–12:30 P.M. | Advisory |
| 12:30–2:10 P.M. | Academic block |

During academic blocks in the morning and afternoon, each team (90 students, 4 subject teachers, and special education support staff) may devise the schedule that works best for the units being taught that week. For example, one week the morning block might be divided into three classes of 50 minutes each—math, science, and English—with the afternoon block providing a long class for each teacher to work on an upcoming interdisciplinary project centered around an exhibition in social studies.

## REFLECTIVE PRACTICE AND THE ROLE OF CRITICAL FRIENDS

Although Jefferson teachers have many of the same staff development opportunities as teachers in traditional schools—for example, teacher workshop days, stipends to attend workshops or conferences, partial tuition reimbursement for college courses—Jefferson promotes continued professional growth of its teaching staff in two unique ways.

First, teachers work together through a variety of regular in-school forums to try out new curricular and instruction ideas and reflect on the impact of their teaching on students' work. Using a process called *curriculum tuning* developed by the Coalition of Essential Schools (Allen, 1995), teachers ask their peers for feedback on emerging ideas for curricular units or analyze the quality of students' work generated in a particular unit. Although some tuning occurs during regularly scheduled team meetings, teachers are increasing their use of this and other action research processes as members of ongoing critical friends groups. Again, borrowing an idea from the Coalition, groups of up to 10 teachers commit to working together for an entire year (meeting after school every other week for a couple of hours) on a vexing education issue such as discipline policy, instruction strategies for heterogeneous classes, evaluation through portfolios, student motivation, or teacher evaluations. Each group is facilitated by one or two Jefferson teachers who have attended an intensive summer institute at Brown University sponsored by the Coalition, and they are provided with coaching by mentors from the Coalition as well.

Second, Jefferson's association with a variety of critical friends brings supplemental funding and expertise into the school to support continual growth and renewal (Olson, 1994). A critical friend is someone from outside the school who is known and respected by the faculty and administration as having expertise in some aspect of education. This person spends considerable time at the school at the invitation of the faculty, not just observing or doing research but becoming actively involved in teaching, curriculum planning, policy discussions, and philosophical debates. The critical friend has no formal power in the school; however, he or she can ask questions as an outsider that staff might not risk and, while carefully maintaining trust and confidentiality, offer different perspectives from those of people embroiled in the day-to-day business of teaching and running the school.

A foreign language teacher's comments about my role as Jefferson's critical friend exemplifies the power of that special relationship:

> Cheryl didn't so much tell us what we should do, she just kept asking questions and guiding us toward finding the answers that would work for us. [She] served as our "roving conscience" relative to inclusion. Because she was present so much in our school, we began to think about how everything we did was going to affect students with disabilities.

Critical friends (from nearby universities or from professional organizations) usually bring financial resources to the school that can be used for professional development. For example, Jefferson's membership in the Coalition of Essential Schools and its participation in a U.S. Department of Education grant (designed to address inclusion and restructuring issues) brought extra funds into the district to enable teachers to spend days away from school planning the curriculum to explore effective instruction methods and develop proficiency standards in their subject areas. These workshops and work days were usually co-facilitated by Jefferson staff and staff from each of the special projects. According to teachers they have been among the most valuable investments of time for professional growth.

## CONCLUSIONS

When casual observers visit Jefferson, many see an education Mecca. Jefferson's accomplishments are remarkable; but, like any organization, it faces a bumpy road ahead as it tries to avoid the seemingly inevitable slide into mediocrity experienced by schools who challenge the education status quo. From my perspective, these challenges include the following:

1.  Maintaining the commitment to inclusion of all students by continually affirming the value of diversity and working to figure out how to provide challenge and support to diverse groups of students
2.  Supporting ever more effective collaboration between general and special education teachers, emphasizing shared ownership, a sane division of labor, and the spirit of cooperation and collaboration
3.  Continuing to grapple with the question, "How can differences in talents and interests be accommodated without sacrificing academic rigor?"
4.  Taking on the challenge of students labeled with emotional disabilities who not only may be struggling within a dysfunctional family but also have been disenfranchised by early, unsuccessful educational experiences. Jefferson must do everything necessary to keep these students in school through individualized scheduling and use of community resources for mentorship,

counseling, and work experiences, without establishing a segregated alternative program.
5.  Maintaining the high level of support for effective professional
    development experiences and keeping their connection to
    emerging issues in the field through continued association with
    respected critical friends

In conclusion,

Jefferson's challenge is to keep the fires of innovation alive without
burning out their teachers; to keep the community involved as active
partners in the school; and, finally, to remember that celebration of
diversity is in everyone's self-interest. We all need to belong in order
to become our own personal best. (Jorgensen et al., 1999)

# 8

# Facilitating and Focusing
# Whole-School Change

Garnett Smith
Robert Stodden
Ronald James
Douglas Fisher
Ian Pumpian

The Individuals with Disabilities Education Act (IDEA) Amendments of 1997 (PL 105-17) added a number of obligations for school systems. High on the list is demonstrable improvement in the long-term results for high school students with disabilities. The list ties these results to enhanced involvement and progress in general education academic curricula (McLaughlin & Verstegen, 1998; Vaughn, Schumm, & Brick, 1998) and to increased participation of these students in general state- and districtwide assessments (Gronna, Jenkins, & Chin-Chance, 1998; PL 105-17, § 614[d]; Vanderwood, McGrew, & Ysseldyke, 1998).

Various national school reforms (e.g., the Goals 2000: Educate America Act of 1994 [PL 103-227], the Improving America's Schools Act of 1994 [PL 103-382], and the School-to-Work Opportunity Act of 1994 [PL 103-239]) have been implemented on the assumption that every aspect of the secondary school instruction system can and will challenge all students academically. The failure, however, to co-ordinate and integrate improvements that accommodate and support students with disabilities to achieve in rigorous, standards-based curricula is particularly troubling (Berliner & Biddle, 1996; Edgar, 1997; Hatch, 1998; U.S. Department of Education, 1995, 1996; Waldron & McLeskey, 1998). The National Longitudinal Transition Study (NLTS) (Blackorby & Wagner, 1996; Wagner & Blackorby, 1996), one of the most comprehensive studies of the long-term outcomes for students with disabilities ever completed, indicated that students with disabilities, the largest percentage of whom have mild disabilities, spend an average of 70% of their school day in general education classrooms, where exposure to the general academic curricula is most common. Although general education placements were positively associated with postschool results, the NLTS also showed that students who were not succeeding in general education courses experienced little postschool benefit (Hocutt, 1996; Wagner & Blackorby, 1996). Ironically, the inclusion of secondary school students with disabilities in general education classrooms, where they are exposed to the general academic curricula, was associated with both better and worse postschool outcomes for these students. It is doubtful that every aspect of the secondary school instruction system is being directed toward the successful involvement and progress of students with disabilities when just getting these students into general education classrooms and to the point of graduation is so difficult (Edgar, 1997; Phelps & Hanley-Maxwell, 1997; Warner, Cheney, & Pienkowski, 1996).

The NLTS study confirms that no magic bullet service or support can consistently aid high school students with disabilities to learn challenging academic content, specifically in core high school courses (e.g., math, science, English, social studies, foreign languages) and to apply that learning to their later postsecondary situations. In 1996, only 19% of high school graduates with disabilities attended some type of postsecondary school within 2 years of leaving high school compared with 53% of their peers without disabilities (Blackorby & Wagner, 1996). Paradoxically, this obsession to seek out magic bullet solutions may inadvertently cause stakeholders to overlook or ignore the substantial body of promising and exemplary special and general education research that exists on successfully providing access to the general curriculum and to learning challenging standards for adolescents with disabilities (Bos, 1995; Carnine, 1997; Cawelti, 1997; Slavin & Braddock, 1994; Waldron & McLeskey, 1998; Warner et al., 1996).

## STANDARDS-BASED CURRICULUM AND THE INDIVIDUALIZED EDUCATION PROGRAM

During the 1990s, the big push in education reform has been to develop new, more rigorous state and district standards for learning. Most standards-based reforms strive to apply the same high standards to all students, including those with disabilities. Although debate continues about the exact nature and extent of these standards, it seems as though a national consensus has been reached about three guiding principles:

1. There will be challenging standards.
2. All students, including those with disabilities, should have the opportunity to strive to meet these challenging standards.
3. Policy makers and educators should be held publicly accountable for every student's performance (Council for Exceptional Children, 1998; McDonnell & McLaughlin, 1997; Wagner, 1998).

For many students with disabilities, the preceding set of principles represents a striking change. Whereas the framework of the standards-based reform stresses accountability for outcomes and applies uniform standards to all students, the legal framework in which students with disabilities have been educated since the 1970s stresses the individualization of goals and instruction and emphasizes accountability for procedural compliance rather than for outcomes. Moreover, many students with disabilities have routinely been excluded from the state and district standards and curriculum (Roach, Fisher, & McGregor, 1996) and from the large-scale assessments that have become the backbone of accountability in standards-based reforms (McDonnell & McLaughlin, 1997).

Clearly, providing appropriate standards-based reforms that include the guiding principles stated previously requires both general and special educators to learn new research-based content and strategies for teaching and assessing students with disabilities. In the broadest terms, the general curriculum amendments in the 1997 IDEA Amendments seek to include students with disabilities in secondary school general education, where, it is hoped, they may be better prepared to make meaningful adult adjustments. Educators routinely fail to align, reference, and ground the process of individualizing goals and instruction exercised through the IEP with the general education program. This historical shortcoming is the reason why standards-based requirements for all students appear to be such a radical change. The fact is that high expectations and standards for all students and the individualization of goals and instruction can be complementary rather than conflictive. Both David Zaino, a special educator (see Chapter 3), and Eileen Bagg-Rizzo, a general educator (see Chapter 4), have come to this decision and have implemented it in practice.

When these processes are not aligned, the capabilities, dispositions, and interests of students with disabilities are often poorly matched to the demands of secondary school environments (Warner et al., 1996). Efforts to incorporate students with varying disabilities into the core high school curriculum have also been hindered by a shortage of financial and professional resources, an inadequate research base, and conceptual ambiguities posed by a firmly entrenched system of grouping by ability that often exposes students with disabilities to dramatically different and unequal levels of curriculum (Jorgensen, 1998; Oakes & Wells, 1998; Vaughn et al., 1998). Aligning standards-based curriculum with individual accommodations and supports requires whole-school changes. Interestingly, Adams,

Jefferson, and Kennedy high schools started at different places in their change efforts. Over time, however, each high school developed schoolwide initiatives to create change and align these two powerful education requirements.

## WHOLE-SCHOOL CHANGE

The Carnegie Foundation Commission advises that piecemeal change may lead to some positive results but is not apt to be as effective as efforts that reach into the various parts of the system, in other words, systemic reform efforts (Cawelti, 1997). The term *systemic reform* has been used to refer to many different ideas and forms. In the fields of general and special education, systemic reform has been referred to in such diverse areas as accountability, least restrictive environments (LREs), equity, and the revision of curriculum content and performance and opportunities standards. In this book, use of the term *systemic reform* focuses on substantially changing the way important components of the high school system interact to improve learning for all students significantly. This definition closely parallels the philosophy of Deming, who defined a system as the organization of two or more interdependent processes or components that work together to accomplish a collective aim (Cawelti, 1997; Dobyns & Crawford-Mason, 1994; Siegel & Byrne, 1994; Wilson & Wright, 1994).

A systems perspective requires change agents to consider causal forces and causal mechanisms. *Causal forces* refers to attitudes and teaching abilities that reside within the high school, whereas *causal mechanisms* refers to the structure of relationships in the schools and the way in which these relationships come to be defined by the system of rules and roles that develops to support them (Schlechty, 1997). In Chapter 2, Sax, Fisher, and Pumpian discuss these forces and mechanisms in terms of the context in which change is attempted. They suggest that this context affects not only the direction and pace of change but also the school change approaches that are selected.

The four approaches to change outlined in Chapter 2 and exemplified in Chapters 5, 6, and 7 are useful in analyzing the ways in which high schools have changed. To examine what has changed, another framework is suggested in this chapter. This framework, based on the work of Cawelti (1997), is discussed in terms of two elements comprising seven critical elements of comprehensive high school systemic reform. Focus elements and facilitating elements include the following emphases:

*Focus Elements*
- Content, performance, and opportunity-to-learn standards
- Effective teaching and active learning
- Results orientation including formative assessment

*Facilitating Elements*
- Technology
- Human resources development
- Shared governance
- Work redesign: Teams and inclusive accomplishments

The conceptual orientation, depicted in Figure 1, implies that typical schools compromise student achievement because they fail to engage in systemic reform. Other schools engage in reform, but they limit achievement because they engage in only the focal elements of change (i.e., activities that provide a focus for the school's transformation) or the facilitating elements of change (i.e., activities that provide technical assistance and supports for the school's transformation). Only schools that address focal and facilitating elements establish conditions that optimize student achievement. Although the case studies of the three schools featured in this book exemplify different approaches, their success became systems change only when all of the elements were attended to and coordinated. It takes more than seat time to improve student achievement. Chapters 2–6 are rich with examples of how attending to these elements led to rich indicators of achievement such as construction of meaning, evaluating information, critical thinking, active learning cooperation, and individualization. A more complete discussion of the seven areas that address focal and facilitating elements of systemic change is provided in the following section. It is hoped that readers will find this discussion useful as a means of reflecting on the previous chapters of this book and on their own change efforts.

## Focus Elements of Systemic Reform

### Content, Performance, and Opportunity-to-Learn Standards
Content, performance, and opportunity-to-learn standards are those research-to-practice elements that deal with the full participation of

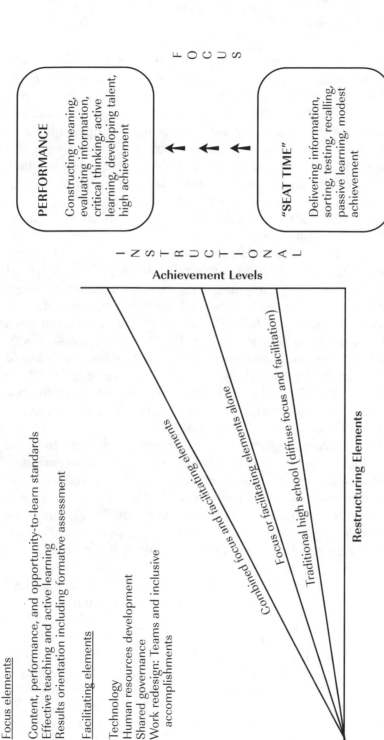

Focus elements

Content, performance, and opportunity-to-learn standards
Effective teaching and active learning
Results orientation including formative assessment

Facilitating elements

Technology
Human resources development
Shared governance
Work redesign: Teams and inclusive
accomplishments

Combined focus and facilitating elements

Focus or facilitating elements alone

Traditional high school (diffuse focus and facilitation)

Restructuring Elements

Achievement Levels

INSTRUCTIONAL

FOCUS

PERFORMANCE

Constructing meaning, evaluating information, critical thinking, active learning, developing talent, high achievement

"SEAT TIME"

Delivering information, sorting, testing, recalling, passive learning, modest achievement

Figure 1.   Seven critical elements of comprehensive high school systemic reform. (Adapted from Cawelti [1997].)

137

all students, including students with disabilities in rigorous core academic and vocational curricula. Elements that embody high-expectation content standards (e.g., what should be taught) are performance standards (e.g., the level of knowledge that students must demonstrate or how well they must perform), and opportunity-to-learn standards (e.g., the context and accommodations necessary to provide students with disabilities with a level playing field in which to achieve content and performance standards) (Council for Exceptional Children, 1998; Gronna et al., 1998; Jorgensen, 1998).

At Kennedy, for example, all students were expected to demonstrate their accomplishments with the Expected Schoolwide Learning Results. These performance standards were key in communicating the expectations that the community had for all students. At Jefferson, each academic teaching team created for students lessons and units that were based on essential questions and expectations for student learning. At Adams, the school-to-work efforts created a new set of expectations that were based on the districtwide expectations for all students. In addition, Adams High School had created content standards for every class. Again, the communication of these expectations and the ability of teachers to create assessment systems so that students could demonstrate their learning were key elements in the evolution of these schools.

***Effective Teaching and Active Learning***   Effective teaching and active learning are those research-to-practice elements that show promise in or exemplify the importance of involving all students in hands-on, problem-based, active learning. These are the messy, exciting, and often frustrating processes by which discoveries are made and inventions are created (Caine & Caine, 1997; Jacobs, 1997). Years of study have provided substantial information on research-based teaching practices as to how to engage students with disabilities more actively in the learning process (Deshler, 1998; Deshler, Ellis, & Lenz, 1996; Mather, 1998; Vaughn et al., 1998). The development of effective teaching elements may hold the highest potential of all seven critical elements for assisting general and special educators, parents, students with disabilities, and other stakeholders to develop their own understanding of the issues involved in standards-based reform and helping them work together to find solutions (Cawelti, 1997; Wagner, 1998).

Effective teaching and active learning were clearly demonstrated at each of the schools discussed in this book. For example, teachers created inclusive units with essential questions at Jefferson. Students were encouraged to discover information about questions with the guidance of their teacher and peers. At Kennedy, a great number of hands-on and applied learning units were developed and implemented. Teachers attribute this to the training they received to teach in a 95-minute block of time. At Adams, students interacted with adults who cared deeply about the career path that they had selected. Students understood English and history, for example, through the lens of tourism and hospitality.

*Results Orientation Including Formative Assessment*   A results orientation including formative assessment is those research-to-practice elements inspired by general and special educators from Dewey to Sizer to Brown. These elements affirm the value of exhibitions of mastery. Schools that are looking to improve achievement through their systemic reforms are not only changing instruction practices but also broadening ways to evaluate student performance and learning. Active learning, service projects, and internships should provide new opportunities to evaluate and document student achievement. Authentic assessments require students to exhibit their learning and be judged by peers, teachers, and community members. Within this context, students with disabilities have the ability to demonstrate their competence and apply their skills to real-life situations and a functional context. Under these circumstances, students can demonstrate their level of achievement with respect to performance and content standards. More important, as Zaino and Pumpian stress in this book, these authentic assessments provide students with an opportunity to demonstrate their learning achievements in important situations and under conditions that involve their use of necessary accommodations and supports. Each of these schools created ways to assess their own progress as well as the progress of their students. All three schools used a form of senior portfolios and exhibitions. These products and events were used to provide students with feedback on their high school career and to inform teachers, parents, and community members about the learning that had occurred.

## Facilitating Elements of Systemic Reform

A general consensus has been reached on the part of national, state, and local education professionals concerning the importance of the three focus elements (high standards, active learning, and a focus on results). Tangible efforts to actually accomplish these systemic reforms, however, have proved difficult to achieve in a busy and comprehensive high school. Traditionally, secondary teachers have been oriented toward teaching academic content and are either untrained or poorly trained in the kinds of developmental and accommodation concerns that enter into planning for students with disabilities. In addition, secondary teachers typically work under stressful and demanding conditions, including large class size; limited time for planning; and limited technical, human, and external resources (Marsal, 1998; Warner et al., 1996). Cawelti stressed, "The enormous challenge involved in school [systemic reform] needs to be recognized if school staffs are to be helped to implement high standards, instruction that motivates students, and ongoing performance assessment that is channeled into improvement efforts" (1997, p. 18). Focal elements of reform are critical, but they will not be implemented unless promising and/or exemplary research-to-practice processes, practices, and resources are identified that facilitate or assist a high school transformation (Cawelti, 1997; Hocutt, 1996; Smith, Edelen-Smith, & Stodden, 1998).

   ***Technology***   Overall, technology is starting to emerge as a significant element in seeking to improve the achievement of students with disabilities in core high school courses. In poll after poll, parents say that technology is essential to a child's education. Many educators believe it is the missing linchpin of school reform (Trotter, 1997). Although it is inappropriate to view technology as a purpose of education (Postman, 1985), technology may be a linchpin to better management, instruction, and performance. In special education, "a 20-year commitment exists to use technology, educational media, and materials to help people with disabilities discover new learning opportunities, communicate effectively, control their environment, and achieve greater mobility" (Hauser & Malouf, 1996, p. 504). Yet, most general and special educators are still more comfortable with chalkboards than with a computer mouse. The element of technology seems critical for general, vocational, and special secondary educators to achieve systemic schoolwide standards-based reform; but, as Kathleen Fulton (1993) from the University of Maryland's Center for Educational Technology pointed out, little is known about using technology to support standards-based reform. Teachers do not learn about this element in their preparation programs. People assume that teachers know content and pedagogy, and teachers are expected to stay up-to-date in those areas. But teachers have not been prepared to think about how research-based technology innovations can enhance teaching (Trotter, 1997). Schools that are committed to improving student achievement must attend to access and availability of new technologies as well as to teacher and student competence in using technology. All three of the schools discussed in this book used educational and assistive technology as adjuncts to instruction. Think about Jamie from Kennedy High School. Her success was due in part to the access that she had to low-technology adaptations provided by her special education team. All classrooms at John Q. Adams High School have computers that are connected to the Internet. The governance team there worked hard to secure funding from the National Science Foundation to complement instruction with technology. Students at Adams can use the Internet to gather information, use e-mail to communicate with others, and use a variety of software programs to complete assignments.

*Human Resources Development*   Research and experience have shown that widespread, sustained implementation of new practices such as increasing the placement and performance of secondary students with disabilities in core high school classes requires a significant amount of planning and training. In Chapter 10, Pumpian addresses this area in detail and reflects on the other chapters of this book with regard to this practice. Time and effort invested in human resources development and support have consistently been shown to have a positive effect on the long-term implementation of innovative instruction models, organizational structures, and administrative procedures (Bos, 1995; McLaughlin & Verstegen, 1998). Indeed, some of the most heartening findings related to schoolwide systemic reform have been from a common report by teachers that some form of human resources development (e.g., technical assistance, summer institutes, preservice and in-service training, critical friend support) had a positive influence on their personal knowledge, attitudes, and teaching practices aimed at enhancing outcomes for students with disabilities (Bandura, 1997; Cawelti, 1997; McLaughlin & Verstegen, 1998; Sagor, 1991; Sparks & Hirsh, 1997).

*Shared Governance*   The third facilitating critical element of this model addresses the importance of developing a shared governance system. New governance systems can provide high schools with the resources, flexibility, and responsibility to unite and support all of the school's stakeholders. These systems facilitate the design and implementation of effective strategies for preparing their high school students to learn the content of the curriculum frameworks to meet a high level of performance (McLaughlin & Verstegen, 1998). In Chapter 2, Sax, Fisher, and Pumpian review the importance of this facilitating element. High school systems do not change themselves. Individuals change systems by acting individually and collectively. Breakthroughs occur when productive connections and networks achieve critical mass and create growing pressure from within for systems to change. At Jefferson, governance strategies that combined central leadership and support (to provide perspective, direction, incentives, team networks, and critical friend monitoring) with local stakeholder control and responsibility (to learn, create, respond, and contribute) resulted in greater overall coherence. The town hall meetings were one way in which this school involved a wide range of people in decisions. At Adams, each career path team made decisions about curriculum and instruction that affected their students. At Kennedy, the shared governance system created greater accountability through the need to obtain support for ideas. For example, when the school decided to investigate a scheduling change, the governance team agreed that 75% of the teachers had to support block schedules before the school would change.

**Work Redesign: Teams and Inclusive Accomplishments**   The American high school is an enduring institution. It has not changed its basic form of organization since the early 1920s. The school day is usually divided into six periods. Lectures, textbooks, teachers' questions and students' answers, paper and pencil, and homework-dominated instruction (Caine & Caine, 1997; Jacobs, 1997). Despite this enduring tradition, a number of high schools that are dedicated to schoolwide standards-based reform are beginning to recognize the need for systematic redesign in schools' organizational work structure (Evans, 1996; Marsal, 1998; Schlechty, 1997; Smith et al., 1998). High schools are reexamining the structure of the day and moving to block schedules to allow longer instruction periods and richer student–adult relationships (Canady & Rettig, 1995). Teaching, learning, and assessment strategies are well beyond "textbook as bible, standardized test as scripture," and "chalk and talk" methodologies. The enduring practices of tracking and ability grouping are also being challenged in this redesign (Jorgensen, 1998; Oakes, 1985; Wheelock, 1992). Teachers and school personnel will not adapt to these revolutionary changes unless they attend to these facilitating elements. The very practice of collaboration inherent in most reforms requires relearning, planning time, and resources. Pumpian (Chapter 10) and Jorgensen (Chapter 7) discuss new roles for specialists and generalists in which special educators bring methods expertise to the classroom and general educators bring content expertise to the classroom. In addition, both Zaino (Chapter 3) and Bagg-Rizzo (Chapter 4) discuss the ways in which their professional lives have changed as they educated students with a variety of abilities and disabilities in the same classroom. These changes have included general and special education teachers working together in teams and being involved with the standards-based decision-making process and the inclusive accomplishment of improved results for high school students with and without disabilities through enhanced learning in the general education curriculum.

## CONCLUSIONS

The teacher reflections and school case studies contained in this book provide perspective and examples of approaches to school change. More specifically, perspectives and examples of systemic inclusive high school reform are provided so that readers may reflect on professional practice and reform efforts. This chapter reflects on these case studies and professional journeys with respect to literature on outcomes and achievement. The book's focus on high school reform ties achievement directly to the postschool outcomes that have been an impetus for special education reform in the 1980s and 1990s. Its focus on achievement also describes the false dichotomy between standards-based curriculum and the IEP that has been created. Last, the approaches to change described and exemplified in this book provide a context for describing a model that aligns significant reform elements with student achievement. To that end, a model based on the work of Cawelti (1997) is described that emphasizes the need to attend to the focal and facilitating elements of systemic change.

# Reflecting on the Least Restrictive Environment Policy

## Curriculum, Instruction, Placement: Three Legs of the Achievement Stool

Virginia Roach

The link between policy and achievement must be considered, especially in response to this book's discussions and examples of inclusive schooling and inclusive school reform. This chapter provides an analysis of the case studies and the teachers' perspectives presented in Chapters 3–7. Specifically, this chapter offers support for the hypothesis that student achievement is dependent on at least three factors: curriculum, instruction, and placement. In 1975, when the Education for All Handicapped Children Act (PL 94-142) was enacted, approximately 2,840,000 children and youth with disabilities were not being provided educational services (National Advisory Committee on the Handicapped, cited in Heward & Orlansky, 1992). Other children with disabilities, although in school, were often in substandard facilities with poorly equipped teachers, learning little beyond basic functional living skills. As a result, one of the major tenets of PL 94-142 was that each student with a disability was entitled to a free appropriate public education (FAPE). The intent, advocates argued, was to ensure better education for students with disabilities by ensuring access to schooling. Yet, as Zaino points out in Chapter 3, although access to schooling is a necessary precursor to student achievement, it is hardly sufficient in and of itself to lead to academic achievement.

## SPECIAL EDUCATION:
## FROM SCHOOL PLACEMENT TO STUDENT ACHIEVEMENT

By the 1980s, it was apparent to families, policy makers, and advocates that the original special education law had not only left the promise of increased student achievement largely unfulfilled but also spawned a separate and vast bureaucracy called special education (National Association of State Boards of Education [NASBE], 1992; Roach, 1991; SRI International, 1990). As special education became a more sophisticated bureaucracy, the field differentiated and specialized (NASBE, 1992), with little regard for the general education program in instruction methodologies, curriculum content, and student placement (Lipsky & Gartner, 1997). Smith and colleagues reviewed this dichotomy in Chapter 7 in their discussion of change and achievement.

As special education became increasingly more isolated within the education enterprise, the outcomes of students with disabilities were systematically monitored nationwide for the first time through annual reports to Congress and other longitudinal studies supported by the federal government. (See Chapter 7 for a review of the data on abysmal postschool outcomes as well as students' lack of access to the general education program or adequate supports within it.)

By the mid-1980s, parents, practitioners, and policy makers became more sophisticated in their understanding of the educational needs of students with disabilities and their academic and social potential. A movement calling for the reintegration of students in special education was developing in the U.S. Department of Education, various advocacy organizations, and many individual families (Wang, 1988). Including students with disabilities in the general education classroom was promoted under the assumption that such placement would enhance student achievement. At the very least, things could not be worse than they were in a segregated special education system. At this point in development, policy and practice discussions focused on the placement of students with disabilities with the notion that placement in the general education classroom in and of itself could support better achievement of students with disabilities. Indeed, a critical body of evidence supports the notion that mere placement in the general education classroom can have a significant and powerful impact on the development of students with disabilities, particularly on their social skills, peer relationships, and communication skills (Kunc, 1992; McGregor & Volgelsberg, 1998). Yet, as Smith and colleagues note in Chapter 7, access to the general education classroom is a necessary precursor to student achievement yet is not sufficient in and of itself to lead to academic achievement.

The calls for integration of the 1980s were replaced by calls for inclusion in the 1990s. Whereas integration focused primarily on student placement, inclusion calls for students with disabilities to be part of (not merely placed in) the general education classroom with adequate supports and services. Concurrent with the move toward inclusion, advocates at the national, federal, state, and local levels stressed the need to focus on the outcomes of students with disabilities, not merely their placement or access to education. The "appropriate" part of FAPE was being reconsidered in light of developments in the field with respect to teaching and assistive technology, cognitive psychology, pedagogy, and brain research. At the same time, as Zaino and others stressed, a sizable portion of the special education community, as well as policy makers in general, continued to focus on maintaining traditional placement models and perpetuating the separate special education bureaucracy.

## GENERAL EDUCATION SCHOOL REFORM: FROM BACK-TO-BASICS TO HIGH STANDARDS FOR ALL STUDENTS

While special education was going through a maturation process,
general education reform efforts also were changing. Contemporary
education reform efforts have been unprecedented in that they have
been unwavering since the release of the watershed report, *A Nation
at Risk*, in 1983 (National Commission on Excellence in Education).
Reform efforts have taken three to four primary foci since the release of this report. Starting from a back-to-basics focus in the early
and mid-1980s, reformers began to chronicle the malaise in U.S. high
schools and propose new approaches to organizing their structure,
culture, and curriculum (Goodlad, 1984; Hirsch, 1987; Sizer, 1992).
Since then, general education reforms have focused on the teaching
and learning process as the operative juncture to enhance student
outcomes (National Commission on Teaching and America's Future
[NCTAF], 1996; Smith & O'Day, 1991). Specifically, standards-based
reform, adopted by the majority of states and local districts, seeks to
establish high, rigorous standards for student achievement while providing greater flexibility to allow those closest to the student the
autonomy needed to structure education programs to best meet student needs (Massell, Kirst, & Hoppe, 1997; Smith & O'Day, 1991).
In addition, the work of the National Board for Professional Teaching Standards and the NCTAF has been influential in focusing education reforms on teacher development, arguing that teacher competence is the single most influential factor—after student background
characteristics—on student achievement (NCTAF, 1996).

In keeping with these education reforms, federal policies have
been systematically aligned to support standards-based reform with
a heavy emphasis on the teaching and learning process. Federal legislation—Goals 2000: Educate America Act of 1994 (PL 103-227) and
Title I of the Improving America's Schools Act of 1994 (PL 103-382)—
was constructed with a heavy emphasis on encouraging states to
develop standards for student achievement, provide professional
development to teachers to support the teaching of those standards,
and develop assessments to measure student progress against those

standards. The U.S. Department of Education (1998) proposal for the reauthorization of Title V of the Higher Education Act (PL 89-329), the Clinton administration's 1999 budget proposal, and discretionary awards made by the Office of Educational Research and Improvement of the U.S. Department of Education all renew the focus on the teaching and learning process, with a heavy emphasis on teacher development as the key to student achievement. The reform policies of the 1980s focused on increasing graduation requirements, student and teacher testing, and new organizational structures for schools. Current efforts focus on curriculum, instructional strategies, and teacher development.

## SPECIAL EDUCATION AND
## GENERAL EDUCATION COME TOGETHER

Although special education and general education reforms have largely been on parallel tracks, both fields have come to focus attention on curriculum and instruction as pivotal aspects of enhancing student achievement. Indeed, as noted in Chapters 2, 5, 6, and 7 of this book, many of the principles that underlie school reform and restructuring are the same principles that underlie inclusive education. The capstone of this new understanding in special education is the Individuals with Disabilities Education Act (IDEA) Amendments of 1997 (PL 105-17). The 1997 IDEA Amendments are designed to support students with disabilities in the standards-based reform efforts of most states and local districts and to align with Goals 2000 and the Improving America's Schools Act. They are based on the premise that the instruction that will be most effective is 1) grounded in the general education curriculum; 2) delivered, to the maximum extent possible, in the general education classroom; and 3) varied and tailored to the unique needs of each student.

The field has changed significantly since the late 1970s. Initially, access to the school was a focus of special education, with the notion that school participation would lead to better student outcomes. Then advocates focused more specifically on access to the general education classroom, that is, integration and inclusion (as a placement issue). Advocates have turned to a more sophisticated notion of inclusion—one that recognizes the interrelated role that curriculum, instruction, and placement play in creating an inclusive school. The case studies in this book discussing Kennedy, Adams, and Jefferson high schools represent model inclusive schools specifically because they are inclusive in each of these core factors.

## CURRICULUM, INSTRUCTION, PLACEMENT: THREE LEGS OF THE ACHIEVEMENT STOOL

Whole-school reform efforts seem to be largely focused at the elementary and middle school levels through such programs as Success for All and Roots and Wings (Tally & Martinez, 1998). Reform strategies such as thematic instruction, writing across the curriculum, and other forms of interdisciplinary instruction are typically easier to implement at the lower grades. This is because 1) younger students are usually with the same teachers the entire day, 2) elementary and middle school teachers are used to teaching more than one subject (for interdisciplinary instruction), and 3) elementary and middle school teachers define themselves as primarily teaching the child as opposed to the subject. Pressing accountability concerns of the typical high school, such as graduation and college entrance requirements, often drive teachers to instruct by using traditional discipline-focused materials, methods, and curricula.

Yet the three high schools highlighted in this book use curriculum, instruction, and placement that are different from those used in the typical high school. This difference creates restructured and reformed schools that focus on the needs of each student rather than on curriculum coverage as paramount. This difference allows for pursuing depth in learning and understanding (Sizer, 1992); it is this difference that creates inclusive schools. The three elements (curriculum, instruction, and placement) create a synergy in these schools to support their entire student bodies. Without any one of the elements, inclusion efforts in these schools likely could not have been adopted as a whole-school philosophy, nor could it be sustained (as Jorgensen points out in Chapter 7) for any period of time.

### Role of Curriculum in Creating Inclusive Schools

One of the tenets of the 1997 IDEA amendments is that students with disabilities must have access to the general curriculum. Not only do the featured schools in this book include students with disabilities in their curricula, but also the curricula themselves are structured to be inclusive. At Kennedy, for example, the curriculum is based on 15 expectations for students (see Chapter 5). The expectations, rather than being organized in the traditional discipline domains of mathematics, English, language arts, science, and so forth, are organized in more global terms according to communications, learning strategies, technology use, responsible citizenship, and work force preparation. Whereas the implicit goal of the traditionally organized high school curriculum is to prepare students for college (hardly an end in and of itself), the explicit goal of the inclusive curriculum is to prepare students for life after high school. Ironically, these innovative programs may provide better college preparation than the college preparation curriculum itself (Rosenstock, 1997)! These goals recognize each student as a lifelong learner (wherever that learning may take place), citizen, and contributing member of society. Because the curriculum itself is geared toward all students in the school with all of their postsecondary school plans, the curriculum itself is inclusive.

Like Kennedy, Jefferson High School operates with a curriculum that is inclusive in nature. Although the learning standards of the school are discipline based, as noted in Chapter 7, student-centered curriculum units and daily lessons are created within those learning standards. The student-centered curriculum (based on an essential question and a final exhibition of student learning) accommodates student differences of all types, including disability, and thus is inclusive.

Of the three schools, Adams High School has probably had the greatest difficulty in transforming the underlying structure of its curriculum. The reform is largely dependent on a Career Pathways curriculum, which has been implemented only partially. Adams has infused two important elements into its curriculum: reading for all students and social justice. Each of these elements has had a direct impact on inclusion in the school. Adams's focus on reading has led to an organizational structure that breaks down the traditional barriers between special and general education. Because an overwhelming majority of students in the school (more than 75%) require additional reading instruction, the general school population has, in essence, been infused into curriculum goals that would typically have been followed only for students in special education at the high school level. Low overall student achievement has blurred the lines between special and general education, reinforcing the notion of one curriculum for all students. These conditions characterize many large inner-city schools. The strength of Adams's approach was not to water down expectations for its student body but to raise them, and two important points related to this fact must be made. First, other schools with similar conditions have not taken the opportunity to become more inclusive. Second, other schools that report high student achievement (e.g., Jefferson High; see Chapter 7) have not depended on these blurred lines of achievement as a basis for their inclusion agenda.

Of the three schools, Adams is the most explicit in adding curriculum topics directly related to social justice and disability. Chapter 6 is replete with examples of how disability topics have been integrated into the curriculum of Adams High School. Disability has been infused into the curriculum through specific lessons on social justice (with disability as the example) as well as through specific lessons on disability itself. In this way, Adams creates an inclusive curriculum through direct understanding of disability issues. This understanding, in turn, creates an ongoing consciousness among the students and staff of including students with disabilities in the curriculum and in campus life.

One of the key elements of inclusion in each of these inclusive, restructured schools is the curriculum. The curriculum design of each school—whether it is based on goals for all students (Kennedy), a student-centered philosophy (Jefferson), or explicit representation of individuals with disabilities (Adams)—is inclusive. The curriculum not only supports the inclusion of all types of students but also helps to maintain the inclusiveness of the core of the school experience.

## Role of Instruction in Creating Inclusive Schools

In addition to creating an inclusive curriculum, all three schools deploy instruction strategies to support all students, including those with disabilities. The instruction strategies support the type of curriculum used in the schools. That is, the instruction methodologies are specific to the curriculum (an approach that is student focused and inclusive) and not so much specific to the individual students (an approach that, in the past, led to highly specialized special education curricula that could not be accommodated in inclusive classrooms). By using the curriculum-specific approach, as noted in Chapter 5, fewer specific modifications are needed and more students can complete assignments "as is." When needed, student-specific instruction modifications are applied for any student, not just for those with individualized education programs (IEPs).

At Kennedy High School, for instance, general education classroom teachers often provide multilevel instruction, which allows all students a variety of ways to demonstrate knowledge. Adapting the lesson for students with disabilities often is not necessary. The school has opted to implement block scheduling, which provides more opportunity for hands-on project work. A critical part of assessment at the school is performance exhibitions that must be completed to develop a student portfolio. This method of assessment allows a greater breadth of demonstrations of achievement than typically allowed in a high school, thus supporting a greater breadth of student capabilities in the curriculum.

At Adams High School, varied instruction, the "commitment to provide a variety of rich educational experiences," is one of the core values of the school. To support this value, Adams provides a variety of opportunities for student learning. The individual tutoring before and after school and the Saturday instruction for focused remediation and extended day courses focus specifically on learning and study strategies that can be applied in the curriculum. Like Kennedy, Adams is experimenting with block scheduling, which has allowed for project-based instruction. Senior portfolios have been phased in at the school, like at Kennedy, allowing for a greater breadth of expression of student achievement. Adams is specifically focused on intensive professional development activities through the use of cognitive coaching to provide peer support as part of instruction strategies (see Chapter 6).

Jefferson's focus on the principles of the Coalition of Essential Schools drives the instruction methods employed in the school. Like Adams, the mission statement of the school embodies a keen emphasis on instruction strategies that are student focused. At Jefferson, according to its mission statement, instruction must be communal and collaborative rather than didactic and hierarchical. At Jefferson, the student is the worker and the teacher is the coach. This conceptualization of student and teacher roles focuses on the student as the creator of meaning in the school. Like Adams and Kennedy, Jefferson uses exhibitions as a means of assessment. At Jefferson, the instruction unit is organized around an essential question that is taught and evaluated through an exhibition. This instruction method, which is consistent with the curriculum at the school, allows for a greater breadth of student performance in the class-room and, hence, is inclusive.

Other instruction methods at Jefferson that support inclusion as well as the curriculum include block scheduling and heteroge-neous grouping. As with the other schools, block scheduling allows teachers the flexibility to go into topics in greater depth, vary in-struction, and provide multilevel instruction. Heterogeneous group-ing supports the notion that the school is untracked and that all students will meet high standards. As mentioned in the previous section, any student is allowed to elect to do an honors challenge within any course. In this way, every student with a disability in the school is enrolled in academic, nontrack courses.

All three schools employ instruction strategies that are inclu-sive of all students. As noted previously, these instruction strategies flow from and are inextricably intertwined with the curriculum of the schools. In addition to inclusive instruction practices such as block sched-uling, heterogeneous grouping, multilevel instruction, and exhibi-tions, each school employs instruction strategies specifically aimed at accommodating the needs of students with disabilities. There is a significant difference, however, between these schools and other schools with more typical special education structures. These schools, through their standard instruction practices, create an environment in which less specific instructional adaptations must be made. In fact, in all three schools, an emphasis is placed on beginning with the lesson as prepared and making accommodations only as needed. This approach is in contrast to traditional special education instruc-tion, which assumes atypicality and adaptation and that students must receive special services to develop new skills (Hitzing, 1980).

## Role of Placement in Creating Inclusive Schools

The third leg of the achievement stool for students with disabilities is placement. With a renewed emphasis on the outcomes for stu-dents with disabilities, not merely on their educational placement, one must explore whether students with disabilities could achieve the outcomes they achieve in these three schools if they were in sepa-rate, segregated classes. If history is any guide, the answer is a re-sounding "No!" (SRI International, 1990). As noted previously, re-search has shown that mere placement in the general education classroom can have a powerful effect on the development of stu-dents with disabilities, particularly in the areas of communication and social development (Kunc, 1992). In inclusive, restructuring schools, however, placement is also the key to academic success, and, as Smith and colleagues (see Chapter 8) note, academic failure in general education is not linked to positive postschool gains.

Students with disabilities in these inclusive, restructuring schools have benefited academically from being included in the general education classroom, curriculum, and instruction. At Kennedy High School, students with disabilities participated in statewide assessments with accommodations for the first time. Over a 2-year period, achievement gains were documented for each student (Rodifer, 1997). The most significant gains occurred in language acquisition (Bagg-Rizzo, 1996). Yet, achievement in these schools also extends to the general student body. For example, recall the reading curriculum that was developed at Adams High School. In a study at Adams High School conducted following their schoolwide efforts at developing an inclusive, restructuring education and reading emphasis, students gained an average of one grade level in achievement in one semester, or about four times what would have been expected given historical trends. Students averaged 137 new vocabulary words and read an average of 5.95 books during the semester (Showers, Joyce, Scanlon, & Schnaubelt, 1998). In addition to the achievement gains, discipline referrals decreased in these schools. At Kennedy, the number of discipline referrals was reduced by 50%, whereas referrals at every other school in the district either increased or remained the same (Jorgensen, Fisher, Sax, & Skoglund, 1998).

The curriculum and the instruction in these three schools are inclusive. If students with disabilities were segregated in these schools, the segregation itself would undermine the curriculum for all students. An inclusive curriculum creates a set of expectations for all students regarding where students with disabilities will be educated. As a student at Adams High School noted, "Changes have been made in my ways of thinking as a result of these activities." In inclusive, restructuring schools, placement of students with disabilities in the general education classroom is related to the achievement of all students, including those with disabilities. Policy makers must examine these issues in terms of a law that, on the one hand, requires bias for general education placement and the availability of necessary supports and accommodations and, on the other hand, requires the availability of a continuum of alternative placements when needed. Specifically, policies should support schools that design comprehensive schoolwide inclusion plans as an appropriate alternative to pull-out, self-contained, and tracking placement strategies. In these cases, the IEP team can focus its efforts on the design and availability of effective supports, accommodations, and services so that students will be successful and well educated.

## CONCLUSIONS

Kennedy, Adams, and Jefferson high schools should be studied carefully because they are all high schools that have restructured the basic teaching and learning process for all students. In each high school, reforms have centered on the curriculum and instruction methodologies instead of on reform elements that are secondary to the teaching and learning process, such as accountability and teacher empowerment. They also bear close scrutiny because they are inclusive high schools as well as restructured high schools. In fact, they could not be inclusive unless they were restructured. Because inclusion encompasses notions of student achievement, not merely student placement, inclusive schools must include students with disabilities in the curriculum. To include students with disabilities in the curriculum successfully requires employment of a variety of instruction methodologies, which these schools have implemented for all students. Last, students with disabilities are an integral part of the full campus experience in inclusive schools. They are in the general education courses, and they participate in other facets of the campus, such as clubs, sports, and special school events. Each of these three elements—curriculum, instruction, and placement—is inextricably intertwined, as illustrated by the three case studies contained in this book. Each element is a necessary and integral part of the other two elements so that no single element can operate on its own. Mere placement is no longer sufficient. Inclusion has evolved from exposure to school to access to the classroom to the participation of students with disabilities as full partners in the educational experience of the school. The challenge for the future is to create more schools like Jefferson, Adams, and Kennedy so that these schools no longer serve as exemplars of unusual excellence but rather as exemplars of the typical high school.

# 10

# Teacher Preparation

## A Long and Winding Road that Leads . . .

Ian Pumpian

For almost 2 decades, I taught classes for teachers who were working toward their teacher certification to work with students with severe disabilities. I started each methods class by informing my students that I knew that none of them had a grandparent who was a teacher who worked with students with severe disabilities. I made this point to emphasize that they were pioneering a new professional field. Keep in mind that President Kennedy requested funds to create a profession of teaching students labeled as having mental retardation. We would be hard pressed to find a teacher who, prior to 1960, was hired to work with students labeled "profoundly (or custodially) retarded." Think about it—the words *teaching, teacher,* and *education* are oxymorons of the words *uneducable, attendant,* and *custodial.*

This book provides reflections of teachers' professional journeys and case studies of high schools engaged in inclusive education reform. Teachers have played a critical role in making schooling more effective and inclusive. The implications for new teacher preparation and ongoing professional development are numerous. Unfortunately, many teacher-training and staff development programs reflect less than contemporary thinking and practice. In this chapter, I propose the need to reconceptualize professional preparation and development programs to be more responsive to schools and to serve as a catalyst for inclusive school reforms in the future. The basis of this conceptualization is the definitions, roles, and relationships used to distinguish "generalists" and "specialists." Although historical traditions in general and special education create a certain level of baggage and stagnation, I believe that historical developments can also provide great insight into professional strengths that can be built upon. First, I review the professional legacies so richly and personally described by David Zaino and Eileen Bagg-Rizzo in Chapters 3 and 4. Next, I suggest that these separate journeys toward inclusive education reform are merging and that the strengths of each professional discipline can be better aligned to improve schools and the education of all students. The role of professional preparation and development programs in fostering this merger and alignment become clear.

## SPECIAL EDUCATION COMES INTO THE COMMUNITY: STRANGERS IN A NEW LAND

Early on, the delivery of special education services was influenced by the principle of normalization (Wolfensberger, 1972). Simply stated, the Golden Rule, "Do unto others as you would have them do unto you," was extended to the disability community. The normalization principle influenced an approach that had been almost exclusively medically oriented to become an approach focusing on education, growth, and change. New teaching technologies, fueled by growing advocacy to apply those technologies, swept through the state institutions and ultimately affected privately supported day programs. At the heart of the deinstitutionalization and normalization movement was strong advocacy from the disability community and from parents and professionals working together. These efforts resulted in unexpected educational achievements realized by people with disabilities. Teachers applied new instruction strategies, and students with severe disabilities began learning a rudimentary set of academic, self-help, and communication skills.

As deinstitutionalization continued, normalization gave way to its new educational synonym, the least restrictive environment (LRE). Day programs in state institutions were moved to public school classrooms. Most students with severe disabilities began receiving services in school buildings designated for special education only or in some other overtly self-contained and segregated fashion. Although the physical environment changed, the curriculum and instruction did not. Teachers continued to use the same content that was developed for institutional wards. It was not until Brown, Nietupski, and Hamre-Nietupski (1976) introduced the criterion of ultimate functioning that the education of students with disabilities was radically and permanently altered. Teachers began making educational decisions within the context of preparing students to function in age-appropriate activities in a wide range of typical environments. Staff education and teacher-training programs responded by designing functional curriculum models. Teachers gained competencies in analyzing various community environments and teaching students skills to engage in important activities that occurred in those environments.

Embedded in this new philosophy of normalization was the principle of partial participation (Baumgart et al., 1980). This principle reinforced the importance of access and identified participation in important activities as a legitimate education outcome. Until that time, students were denied access to many environments and activities if it was determined that independent mastery was not a likely outcome. The goal of participation reinforced the need for teachers to build competence in designing adaptations and accommodations and in individualizing instruction. Students responded to the creativity and competencies of their teachers by exceeding former expectations. Students' access to new environments, activities, and other possibilities continued to expand.

As students gained access to new places and opportunities, their families and teachers faced new roles, responsibilities, and challenges. First, parents' roles in the education decision-making process changed. At least in progressive programs, they became welcomed partners in selecting and prioritizing important places and activities for instruction. Even when their partnership was not welcomed, parents learned to invoke their due process rights and utilize advocacy networks to influence education designs. In response, teachers began to develop competencies for collaborating more effectively with parents as education partners. Teachers also were required to learn a new set of local, state, and national rules and regulations and how these affected students and schools. Second, as students with disabilities gained access to more environments and activities, they also began interacting with peers with and without disabilities. Teachers began to develop competencies in analyzing and supporting different types of social and academic relationships.

Another result of gaining access to more environments led to the design of specific strategies for teaching functional skills in those environments. The introduction of community-based instruction (Falvey, 1995) established the precedent for teaching and learning to occur outside the special education school site—that is, to occur in the environments in which the skills would ultimately be used. Not long after that, classrooms for students with severe disabilities were opened on elementary and high school campuses, reducing the number of special education–only schools. The predominant service delivery model continued to be self-contained classrooms often located in physically separated wings of the school. In this service model, off-campus or community-based instruction continued, and opportunities for students to visit and learn in general education classrooms were gradually initiated. This practice of inclusion was typically limited to students who had less significant disabilities and, most often, to those whose parents demanded these experiences. Only what were considered the most progressive programs offered these opportunities as part of the curriculum.

Special education teachers had learned a new set of negotiation skills as they facilitated students' access to a variety of recreation, work, and community environments. They were able to enhance those negotiation skills further when they began to include students with disabilities in general education classrooms. Clearly, this new focus influenced teachers such as David Zaino and Eileen Bagg-Rizzo, and it set the direction for staff development and teacher preparation. New skills and instruction strategies were introduced, knowledge bases were expanded, and philosophical foundations were challenged. It was also a period when teacher-training programs seemed to limit the time and attention devoted to studying the field's "deinstitutional" roots—roots that unified teachers and advocates with cause and reason to move away from and be wary of all forms of segregation. Ironically, in the late 1990s, controversy and resistance follow any scrutiny of self-contained classrooms and poorly supported mainstream placements as newer versions of segregation. Why are newer, more subtle forms of segregation tolerated and supported by those who worked so hard to end blatant forms of exclusion and segregation?

The increase in and viability of more inclusive education practices has shifted the focus of the debate about segregation from, "Why should we include students with disabilities?" to, "How do we do it better?" No longer solely a theoretical debate, the consideration of how to teach all children is an essential component of contemporary education policy and practice. As a result, teachers continue to have a critical role in the school change process. Their understanding of, competence in, and contributions to the change process are essential. Zaino, as well as many of his contemporaries, gained much of his competence through the school of hard knocks and experience. It is hoped that teacher-training programs will do a better job of preparing future special education professionals to feel less like strangers in this land we call public school. Teachers such as Zaino have become welcomed strangers, if not fully assimilated immigrants, through hard work, the formulation of strategic alliances, and competence in teaching and learning. The next section considers how the preparation of the new generation of teachers can be improved.

## CHALLENGES FOR PREPARING GENERAL EDUCATORS: LET THE PAINTERS PAINT

Curriculum and pedagogy, rather than using the lived experience of students as a foundation, have been based on what can be described as alien and imposed reality. The rich experiences of millions of our students, and their parents, grandparents, and neighbors, have been kept strangely quiet. (Nieto, 1996, p. 3)

Eileen Bagg-Rizzo (in Chapter 4) thought that as a teacher she would look out and see a class similar in appearance to the ones she had sat in as a child. Perhaps she expected fashions to change, but never did she imagine such diversity among her students. If the descriptor of her childhood classroom was "homogeneous," then "heterogeneous" describes the classrooms in which she teaches today. Overall, the student population is becoming more diverse, both ethnically and linguistically. The vast majority of children educated in the United States live in large cities. Seventy-five percent of inner-city youth are non-Caucasian. Children in these multiethnic communities speak more than 150 languages, with more than 15% of the students being classified as English language learners (Sautter, 1994). Enormous disparity exists in the educational achievement curves of these youth as compared with their suburban peers. The heterogeneity of teachers, however, has not kept pace with the increased diversity of students (Nieto, 1996). Despite the gross overrepresentation of African American students placed in special education (England, Stewart, & Meier, 1990), the percentage of the nation's African American teachers is expected to decline (Action Council on Minority Education, 1990). The teacher mobility rate in many inner-city schools exceeds 30%, suggesting that new teachers pay their dues before "earning their way" to the much sought after affluent school assignments or, too often, leave the profession.

Some teachers attempt to use seniority and suburban job offers to avoid confronting the reality of the growing diversity of the student population. Other teachers use identification and referral processes to remove the reality of that diversity from their classrooms. Tracking, sheltering, and self-containing groups of students further preserve the myth that classroom homogeneity can exist. This myth clouds the awareness of diversity. The reality is that many minorities constitute the majority and that new diagnoses (e.g., attention-deficit/hyperactivity disorder) are leading to large percentages of the population being labeled. If left unchecked, the smallest group of students in the school may be those in the general education program. For example, schools in Boston are referring more and more students to special education, at a rate of 22%, to get students the help that they need. "If all Chapter 1 and special education students returned to the regular classroom, the districtwide ratio would fall by 6, from 22.7 students for every teacher to 16.6" (Miles, 1995, p. 481).

Undoubtedly, poverty exacerbates the issues of providing a quality education; however, we have a tendency to reminisce about the lost golden age of education. Readers are referred to Schorr (1997) for a more comprehensive look at the myth of the golden age of education. Such an age simply did not exist. In the past, rates of educational success, failure, and achievements were no different from those of today, even though we had managed to exclude or deny access to 30% of the school-age population (Schorr, 1997). Not only were educational achievements no greater in the past than they are today, but also public schools reflected antidemocratic principles related to race, religion, culture, and ability. Attitudes, policies, and practices of the past that linger for many adults today, in my opinion, create one of the biggest barriers to reform and change. We have the chance to reflect and demonstrate a more balanced set of public attitudes, policies, and practices to the next generation of adults. The best of public education is before us, not left behind.

Sooner or later, in the majority of schools and classrooms across the United States, teachers will not be able to deny the diversity of their students. Fortunately, growing numbers of teachers have learned the futility of such behavior and have moved to accept the new portrait of the typical American classroom. Acceptance does not guarantee success in and of itself. If teachers continue to use old and outdated curricula and instruction strategies and fail to acquire appropriate supports and resources, they will only perpetuate a good idea executed poorly. It is these circumstances that led Kunc (1997) to remark, "Inclusion does not cause dysfunction; it exposes it." Such circumstances are not inevitable, however, as many teachers learn to accept and appreciate student diversity by valuing what every student brings to the learning situation. They, like Bagg-Rizzo, may not have had the opportunity as a child, or even as a student teacher, to experience this diversity. But they learned, as did Bagg-Rizzo, that they could use these circumstances to enrich the teaching and learning occurring in their classrooms.

When Bagg-Rizzo looked out at her class and saw faces and behaviors that she did not expect to see, she realized that this was her class and that she had the fortune, opportunity, and responsibility to share with them her passion for teaching and learning. She did not accept this reality naively. The value that she placed in herself as a lifelong learner became evident. She participated in but did not limit herself to the staff development offered to all teachers in her district and school. She recognized the cultural and linguistic diversity of her students and chose to go back to the university to earn certification in cross-cultural language and academic development. As the interest in and later commitment to inclusive educational placement and support practices developed, she pursued her master's degree in special education. She carefully selected a program that allowed her the opportunity to concentrate her studies within her content area, English, and enhance that mastery with a pedagogy that focused on individual accommodations, peer interactions, and a full range of appropriate support strategies. She also picked a program that emphasized participatory action research (Stringer, 1996), thus connecting her studies to the interest and responsibility that she assumed for education innovation and reform at her school. Her action research reinforced a collaborative model of change and provided her with new colleagues, resources, and alliances that had a direct impact on her school and her classroom. Her graduate studies and school reform work strengthened her relationship with colleagues that resulted in attending, and later presenting at, a variety of professional conferences. It also led to her reflective and constructive chapter in this book.

Bagg-Rizzo looked out at the portrait of her class and realized her early education experiences had not fully prepared her to appreciate its artistic beauty and nuances. She could have rejected the canvas in search of a more familiar one; instead, she added new techniques and brushes to the passion and mastery she had already acquired. Arguably, her preparation should have included more history and appreciation related to her art of teaching; a two-unit course in inclusion did not scratch the surface of what she needed to know to integrate and infuse her introductory methods and practical experiences throughout her classes. As schools become more inclusive, children will experience diversity much earlier than did this particular English teacher and her contemporaries. The strategies that this book describes throughout are meant to enhance the appreciation and value that children hold for that diversity. Bagg-Rizzo illustrates how constructive a professional growth plan, a healthy attitude, and a passion for the art of teaching can be in attenuating the limitations of earlier teacher preparation. She learned to use her entire painter's palette to construct new pictures and to paint with all of her students and colleagues. Her art is deeper, richer, and more beautiful than she ever imagined it would be.

## CHALLENGES FOR PREPARING EDUCATORS: AN AMERICAN PATCHWORK QUILT

> If the interweavings of a truly inclusive neighborhood could be depicted by a colorful piece of fabric, one would find the vivid, colorful threads woven by people with disabilities in that fabric too. (Perske, 1993, p. 2)

Progressive special educators like David Zaino and his contemporaries bring important competencies to their schools in the attempt to meet the educational needs of the entire student body. These educators should have knowledge, experience, and competencies in the following areas:

- Complying with legal and procedural requirements
- Encouraging parent involvement and collaboration
- Negotiating community and business partnerships
- Designing accommodations and adaptations to individualize or enrich curriculum, instruction, and assessment
- Infusing basic and functional skills into age-appropriate activities and routines
- Creating strategies to proactively respond to various intellectual, physical, and behavior challenges
- Facilitating communication and social interaction skills and peer supports

Certainly, many special education teacher training programs have not provided future teachers with such knowledge, experience, or competencies. Some programs have even reinforced a contradictory set of skills and values. These competencies, however, are consistent with the progressive legacy of special education policy and practice. This legacy has led special educators like Zaino to adopt a more inclusive agenda of educational change and reform. Both the legacy and the agenda hold further implications for teacher-training and staff development programs, including the initiation of innovative forms of collaboration among specialists and their general education counterparts and the analysis of the roles that special educators can play in curriculum and instruction as well as in systems change efforts. Consistent with the definitions of disability as reviewed by Zaino, further implications stress the need for designing classrooms that will ultimately lead to a more inclusive society.

What about the legacy and agenda for the general educator? Bagg-Rizzo's teacher preparation provided her with the opportunity to develop her content mastery. She understood her subject matter and was well prepared to participate in and lead any number of committees dealing with content standards and curriculum framework. As she began teaching, her district's staff development increasingly provided her with access to new information, resources, and technologies. She participates in reviewing, prioritizing, implementing, and evaluating a variety of educational reforms and initiatives as her district and school are challenged by issues of assessment and accountability. The democratic legacy of progressive public school education prepared Bagg-Rizzo and her peers to undertake these challenges. Similar to special education teacher-training programs, general education teacher-training and staff development programs have certainly reinforced contradictory values and skills. The legacy of public education, however, depends on reform that promotes democratic values and an informed and well-prepared citizenry. This legacy has led general educators like Bagg-Rizzo to realize that schools must be models of democracy (Glickman, 1993) and, therefore, that the educational reform agenda must be effective, responsive, and inclusive. A general education legacy and agenda also have obvious implications for teacher-training and staff development programs that recognize new forms of collaboration required to move to a more inclusive society.

Such collaboration implies not only new relationships among general and special educators but also a need for more common ground—that is, a shared set of knowledge, values, and competencies between the two groups of professionals. It would be difficult to find educators more committed to developing this common ground than Zaino and Bagg-Rizzo. Professional growth, however, must be grounded more firmly in professional preparation and development programs and not dependent only on individual discovery and commitment. When the skills, interests, and passions of the Zainos and Bagg-Rizzos of the teaching world come together in schools and classrooms, new and impressive quilts are woven with beautiful fabric that reflects the teaching and learning of a community.

We have been sensitive to those who claim that including students with disabilities in general education classrooms is primarily for social reasons. We are quick to counter such allegations with ample examples of significant and unexpected academic skills and gains. My colleagues and I have a good friend who employs a woman who receives specialized supported employment services because of her disabilities. One day, this individual confessed to us that he finally understood why we have worked so hard to promote inclusive education. He said that his employee has helped him realize how important social skills are to job success, and he concluded that he believes that we promote inclusive education because it provides ongoing opportunities for people with and without disabilities to learn and experience interacting socially and effectively with each other. My colleague was quick to counter our stressing the relationship between traditional academic gains and inclusive educational placements. Our employer friend listened patiently, then shook his head and responded, "It's relationships. . . . It's all about relationships."

## FACING THE CHALLENGES
## TOGETHER: A BRAVE NEW WORLD

The changes in society and those wrought by inclusive education that are highlighted in this book have occurred in a new world, one that I did not experience as a student. Advances in information technology have had a strong impact on society. Americans enjoy the fastest, most efficient, most accessible press and communication system the world has ever known. A free press is one of our most formidable rights and protections. Unfortunately, American society tends to appreciate the press's ability to be quick more than its ability to deliver comprehensive, insightful information. Stated another way, Americans tend to rely more on the headline than the article and on the sound byte more than the speech. Similarly, the effectiveness of education is evaluated on the basis of specific test scores and comparison of those scores. The public and the school officials who respond to them often rely exclusively on these scores and comparisons because they are simple and quick indicators of performance. As a result, other, perhaps more informative, indicators of effectiveness are ignored because results can be collected only over time, they may require more sophisticated understanding, or they do not lend themselves to quantitative analysis or comparison. The act of holding educators accountable gets watered down to teaching to the test, and then the balance between content standards and performance standards is disturbed. The ability to teach for understanding and depth versus teaching to the textbook is thwarted, and attention to personal and interpersonal skills and behaviors takes a back seat to performance of more rote and measurable skills. Ironically, it was the business community, when asked by the Department of Labor (Secretary's Commission on Achieving Necessary Skills, 1992), that stressed the need and importance for graduates to leave school with a set of skills and behaviors beyond the range of those measured by the tests (and test scores) on which the public relies and by which the public measures schools' success. Teachers must appreciate the need to prepare students to take a battery of revised tests, but they must also be able to resist merely teaching to the test. They must be individually and collectively prepared to communicate and work with supervisors, parents, and the community at large to establish and highlight other important measures of student success and school effectiveness. Parents and teachers must understand that, as President Franklin D. Roosevelt once said, "The only limit of our realization of tomorrow will be our doubts of today. Let us move forward with strong and active faith."

Although others might assume that merging general and special education teacher preparation and professional development will result in an elimination of specialty, I do not. I promote the creation of a much more comprehensively prepared education generalist (in both preservice and in-service programs), based on the assumption that each generalist must also be prepared and developed as a specialist. Some teachers develop their specialties in curricular content pedagogy and mastery (i.e., general educators), and others will develop their specialties in methods of instructional delivery and pedagogy (i.e., special educators). The challenge is to broaden the common ground of the generalists and enrich the competencies of the specialists in the professional development and growth of both new and veteran teachers (see Chapter 7 for a sample of new job descriptions).

Educators who share a common, comprehensive set of educational competencies find themselves better prepared to collaborate and complement each other's more specialized training skills and responsibilities. It seems fair to expect that general educators bring content expertise to the learning situation and special educators bring methods expertise and individualization strategies. The functional boundaries between these broad areas of expertise are nonlinear and fluid and are likely to diminish over time with experience and adequate staff development and collaboration. Teachers who fail to develop and demonstrate some level of content and methods expertise are unable to maintain effectiveness with their students or credibility with other teachers, administrators, and parents.

Inclusive education reform is not about compromising one student's (or one group of students') education for another, nor is it a blind endorsement of placing and grouping students without attention to the supports that students and teachers need to create an effective learning environment. Instead, such reform assumes that children can receive a quality education in a nontracked system if the resources and services to educate all of those children are well coordinated and effectively delivered.

Proponents believe effective inclusive schooling models can prepare students to participate and contribute to democratic values and society. Reforms would likely lead to the consideration of multiple learning environments; creative instruction arrangements, strategies, and accommodations; and appropriate assessments of student performance that promote teaching and learning. Numerous examples of these innovations are provided throughout this book. Reforms should focus attention on formidable content and performance standards. Teachers must be able to understand, articulate, and contribute to negotiating these standards. Teachers always have played and will continue to play a pivotal role in making curriculum and instruction decisions. They also assume a pivotal role in determining the direction and pace of curricular reforms.

## LOOKING FORWARD: ON THE ROAD AGAIN

Despite reports of national commissions, despite state mandates, and despite carefully engineered and expertly driven change strategies, it is the 2.2 million teachers that account for 26 billion teacher–student contact hours in schools that will, in the end, decide what happens to students. (Sergiovanni, 1996, p. 156)

Clearly, teachers make a difference. But for teachers to continue to make a difference in the lives of their students, their preservice and in-service education and training must change to meet students' changing needs. Special educators have a rich history of developing and promoting social interactions. Their ability to establish peer supports and effective communication systems is a valuable asset to enhancing inclusive educational practices. General educators recognize the importance of social relationships for their students, but they have had less training in how to develop these relationships and supports than have their special education counterparts. All teachers who have and share these competencies will complement the constructivist, cooperative, and democratic concepts and practices highlighted throughout this book. Competencies related to social interaction, peer supports, and cooperative projects must be stressed in teacher preparation and professional development.

Douglas Fisher, Caren Sax, and I argue in Chapter 2 that teachers must be knowledgeable about system change and the change process. Chapters 5–7 advance this argument with the conclusion that teachers must be competent participants in the change process. Teachers need to recognize how their schools and districts are approaching change, what the strengths and limitations of those approaches are, and how to positively influence the change process. I wonder whether teacher-training programs will consider such competencies as commissions write the standards for teacher credentials and certification and as states design ways to test minimal teacher competency. If programs fail to address teachers' roles as change agents, how will they manage, let alone survive, the chaos?

## CONCLUSIONS

In conclusion, I borrow Eileen Bagg-Rizzo's artistic metaphor one final time: Teacher preparation and staff development programs must continue to set up the easel, position the lighting, and place the paints on the palette. Teachers and students will, as they always have, respond creatively, productively, and effectively to the challenges and opportunities of public education. The portrait of progressive public schooling need know no upper limits or prevent any child from realizing its importance.

# 11

# Families

## The Key to Continuity

Barbara Buswell

This book is about change—change on a personal level and change on a systems level. Each of the people and schools described in this book has experienced significant development and has become more inclusive in the process. In addition to the significant changes highlighted in this book, continuity emerged as an important consideration. Continuity is one of the underlying and possibly undefined themes in this book. The stability and continuity that Sax, Fisher, and Pumpian write about in Chapter 2 are critical to the change processes, and it is fascinating that both change and stability had to coexist so that all students could achieve and prosper.

The final chapter of this book is written from the perspective of a parent. You met one of my children, Wilson, in the foreword of this book, in which he and his friend Aaron write about their experiences in Washington Close-Up. Along with 300 other high school students from across the United States, Wilson and Aaron experienced a week in Washington, D.C. They met members of Congress, interacted with federal agency staff members, and visited a number of historic sites. Washington Close-Up was one of those magical times for Wilson. You see, he had back surgery a year before the trip and had experienced a number of complications related to the surgery. One night at Children's Hospital, he looked over to me as if he wanted to talk. When I asked him if he needed something, he blinked to say "Yes." I asked if he was hungry, and he blinked "No." I asked if he needed suctioning, and again he blinked "No." I asked if he needed a pain pill; again, "No." When I asked if he needed someone to read with him, he blinked "Yes!" He wanted to keep up in school and get back to the friends and the activities he missed so much. He wanted to graduate on time as a senior with his class.

Although I have told this story more times than I can count, each time I retell it I learn something new. As Wilson grows older and his needs and dreams change, I am realizing more fully the importance of continuity in maintaining commonly held values, sustaining the relationships within and outside our family, and communicating with others who have essential roles to play in Wilson's life. In this chapter, I discuss the meaning of inclusion for families, the family's role in establishing and safeguarding continuity, and how families hold the key to well-planned transitions. As part of my responsibility for closing this book, I end with suggestions for families and educators as they experience the ebb and flow of inclusive education. I offer these suggestions as my son leaves his high school for the world of higher education.

## MEANING OF INCLUSION FOR FAMILIES: WHAT DO WE ALREADY KNOW?

> When parents are asked what goals they have for their children with disabilities, their response, as one parent said, is that "our goals are no different for our children with disabilities than they are for our other children." Parents want all their children to grow up to be happy, contributing members of society, able to interact with the community, to feel good about themselves, and to be valued by others. (National Association of State Boards of Education [NASBE] Study Group on Special Education, 1995, p. 37)

In their study of parent perspectives, Erwin and Soodak (1995) interviewed nine parents from New York. These parents were selected because of their desire for inclusive education. Each of the parents was asked four questions:

1. How did your child's educational placement come about?
2. How do you define inclusion?
3. What were your experiences in pursuing inclusive education?
4. How did the process of pursuing inclusion affect you?

Data from the interviews revealed three common themes: the important meaning inclusion has had in the family's life, gaining access to inclusive education, and positive personal transformations.

This group of parents forwarded several beliefs and ideas about inclusive education and its impact on the family. The researchers classified these stories under the heading "Meaning of Inclusion." As a group, the parents indicated that inclusive education increased their children's sense of belonging. They also maintained that inclusive education was a right and that all children should have the same opportunities and experiences. The parents also were supportive, however, of those families who do not choose inclusive education, and they were unwilling to force their beliefs onto others. The group was clear that the decision-making process should involve family members. Each of these beliefs has been documented elsewhere in the professional literature (Falvey, 1995; NASBE Study Group on

Special Education, 1995; Stainback, Stainback, & Forest, 1989; Strully & Strully, 1989).

The second theme, gaining access to inclusive education, generated a great deal of discussion about negotiating a complex system. Parents viewed their experience as a journey, and they noted the difficulties in implementing inclusive education. McAnaney (1992) and Zipper, Hinton, Weil, and Rounds (1993) have documented similar experiences for families.

This study also emphasized parents' personal transformations. Parents seemed to feel that they were forced into advocate roles and were pleased when they were able to develop parent–professional partnerships and share the responsibility for their children's education. A number of other researchers have emphasized these partnerships, including Salisbury (1992), Turnbull and Turnbull (1997), and Zipper et al. (1993).

In another study of parents' perceptions regarding the inclusion of their children with moderate or severe disabilities, Ryndak, Downing, Jacqueline, and Morrison (1995) analyzed 13 audiotaped interviews with parents. Specifically, this study examined parents' perceptions of "(a) skills acquired by their children after receiving educational services in inclusive settings, (b) the most significant benefit of inclusive services for their children, and (c) their vision for their child's future following inclusive educational services" (Ryndak et al., 1995, p. 148). Each of the students represented in this study received special education services within general education classes. Prior to inclusion, however, all had been educated in a special day class.

Parents perceived a number of academic, social, and communication benefits from their child's membership in an age-appropriate general education classroom. In addition, parents reported that their children displayed more appropriate behavior and positive attitudes when they were with peers without disabilities. This study complements the growing body of research regarding parents' attitudes, beliefs, and perceptions on inclusive education (Fisher, 1996; Guralnick, 1994; Miller et al., 1992).

Another study on parents' perspectives was conducted by York and Tundidor (1995). These researchers conducted 45 focus groups with a total of 335 individuals. Of these, 112 were faculty members or administrators, 80 were parents, 79 were support personnel, and 64 were students. In addition to the numerous benefits, the adults in this study identified several barriers to and priorities for change, including negative attitudes, typical student academic progress, rigid general education curricula, insufficient time for collaboration, insufficient funds for staffing and materials, and the need for increased parent communication and involvement. The authors noted that the responses were consistent across adults, with one exception: Parents specifically voiced concern for their children's safety and the protections that were available in general education classes.

These concerns need to be considered and addressed as schools begin to implement inclusive education curricula. It is clear from this research that parents are supportive of inclusive education but that they want school systems that are skilled, responsive to their needs, and willing to work in collaboration with the families' priorities. Establishing a collaborative relationship requires a certain level of trust and respect that cannot be presumed. The following excerpt from *Winning Ways* explains why achieving this relationship continues to be a challenge:

> Thorough planning and strong lines of communication are the foundation for building a mutually trusting and respectful relationship between parents and educators. As with any aspect of education, both parents and teachers need to feel they can work together to support children. Unfortunately, when it comes to parents of students with disabilities, many teachers have preconceived notions of how "unrealistic" these parents are, how "demanding" they are, or how "generally uncooperative" they are as a group. (NASBE Study Group on Special Education, 1995, p. 39)

Given all that is known about parents and their interest in obtaining the best education possible for their children, the desire for their children to be members of the school community, and the successes that students with and without disabilities experience in inclusive schools, why do service delivery teams still struggle during annual changes?

## CONTINUITY

How do teachers, families, and other school personnel work together to establish and maintain continuity for students, who face a variety of changes every year (i.e., from one grade level to the next, from one school to another, and from one support team to another)? With every transition, a new composition of teachers, aides, related-services providers (e.g., occupational and physical therapists, speech-language specialists, nurses), and peers too often start over in learning how to provide the most appropriate supports to students, particularly to those students with the most significant disabilities. Searching for appropriate supports by trial and error takes precious time away from addressing new goals. Although cumulative records accompany students, sometimes the most essential information that previous teams learned does not transfer easily into documents. Challenges that were once overcome are often faced again. If the new team does not know the student, then the student flounders, parents become upset, and people on the new team sometimes begin questioning why this student is included in their classroom or in their school. General education teachers frequently report frustrations when they perceive that they are expected to know how to teach or support a student but feel that they lack the necessary experience, information, and training to do so. This frustration is more obvious at the secondary level, when students have different teachers for every class and often have different support staff throughout the day. Without proactive planning and effective communication, students become vulnerable. The intentional transfer of knowledge, information, and support is critical to prevent reactive situations from occurring. How many times have you heard teachers say, "I wish someone could just send the right information about a student so we don't have to reinvent the wheel"? Then they proceed to reinvent not only the wheel but also the axle, the body, the transmission, and sometimes the whole car!

## Roadblocks to Continuity

Why are transition and articulation of crucial information so complicated and difficult? First, a variety of service delivery and support paradigms exist at different schools and specific grade levels. Often a student who has been successful at one grade level encounters a new way of being provided resources and supports at the new level. Unfortunately, the change is not always for the better. Second, supporting students in inclusive classrooms requires individualized and unique support approaches. These approaches may change from year to year, and what may work for one team may not be successful for another. A third complication in the transition process can be attributed to inadequate or nonexistent in-service training and technical assistance and consultation. Staff need immediate information and strategies during the first few weeks of school, when school personnel are typically busy and resources are not easily accessible or available. If no professionals with time and expertise are available to assist or be proactive at the beginning of the year, students suffer. No one feels ownership of or responsibility for the students' programming or support, and, at that point, few are likely to volunteer to assume such responsibility. Consequently, as parents watch their child flounder early in the year, perhaps after having had a successful experience previously, they become frustrated. In response, many parents force the issue and are then labeled as pushy and adversarial by teachers and administrators.

Parents then turn to the student's individualized education program (IEP) as a compliance tool rather than as a road map for their child's individualized support. In the end, families are in conflict with schools, and the very approach that would help the child be successful is sabotaged. Most parents prefer to work collaboratively with the school team to support the child, but many feel that this route is impossible when they are forced to compromise their child's situation because of service delivery practices that do not work. Furthermore, when inclusion is being approached for one student at a time rather than in a broad, systemic way, each family must fight its own battle, leaving little changed for the families who follow.

## Strategies for Success

What strategies can be used to ensure continuity for students with significant disabilities in inclusive schools? The most effective strategies are implemented simultaneously, both the "top-down strategies" (i.e., those used by administrators) and the "bottom-up approach" (i.e., strategies used by members of the team sending the student to the new situation, the team receiving the student, and the family).

*Administrators' Roles*    What can administrators do at the district and building levels? First, as discussed in previous chapters, they can frame inclusive education in terms of general education reform and recommended practices. In this way, the likelihood increases that the people in the new school will understand and embrace the importance of broadening instruction approaches and curricula to encompass a diverse learner. Second, instead of viewing special educators as teachers of special children, administrators can reframe teachers' roles as those of inclusion facilitators or of people who assist children to be successful in general education classrooms.

Next, administrators can ensure that multiple opportunities for in-service training are available and that access to resources is a priority. Administrators can also identify or develop staff at the district level who have the skill and experience to troubleshoot when challenges occur. Depending on their own skills and experience, administrators may coach classroom teachers on the implementation of effective strategies.

A critical role for administrators at the building and district levels is to hire teachers and support staff with an understanding that they will accept an inclusive schooling paradigm. If staff need to be hired to support a particular student, it is important to include the family and the successful teacher from the previous school to help identify a person who has the skills to be effective in this role. Administrators can also find in the grade, the school, or the department that the student is entering key people who are receptive, proactive educators who will most likely develop ways to support the student successfully. Finally, administrators must view transition strategies for students from one year to the next as a priority. They can encourage staff to be proactive in learning as much as they can from the sending team so that in the fall both students and teachers feel comfortable and the potential for success is well established.

*Sending and Receiving Teams*   Strategies for the sending and receiving teams that have formed around an individual student include thoughtful planning and an expectation that the planning will be implemented. Each team develops a plan of what needs to be accomplished and by when. Although the end of a school year is hectic at best, planning must be initiated before the school year ends and resumed before the following school year begins. The sending team should document approaches and strategies that have worked well in supporting the student. In addition, they can interview and document information from key people who supported the student successfully or who understood the strategies that helped bring about the student's successes. Whether recording this information on audiotape, on videotape, or in notebooks, receiving input from classroom teachers, specialists, and classmates and peers of the student is essential. A further helpful step that teams report is to make available to the sending and receiving team members an opportunity to observe each other's classrooms to see how the student responds in different situations. Finally, one of the richest information resources is the expertise and knowledge of the student's family.

*Families*   Families can be instrumental in developing a record of successful strategies for the new team to have as a reminder when they get stuck. One way to do this is to create a transition booklet. A transition booklet can be a document for people to use to learn about critical strengths-based information as well as supports that work. It can also be a training tool. If the team decides to create a transition booklet, there are some pitfalls to avoid in terms of what should and should not be included. Transition booklets should include the following kinds of information:

1.   Descriptions of the student that are positive
2.   A student profile describing the student's strengths, interests, favorite activities, and IEP goals or learning priorities for the year, as well as other unique information that classroom teachers need to know
3.   A list of tasks that a teacher assistant or an aide completes, defining their roles in relation to the student and to the teacher (In addition, the ad for the aide position should be included, describing the personal qualities desired by the student should another person need to be hired in the future.)
4.   Pointers about physical assistance that the student may need
5.   Tips on communicating with the student, particularly if the student has difficulty in expressing him- or herself or if the people around the student have difficulty in understanding the student
6.   Behavioral supports that work and a description of situations to avoid or ways to structure situations to eliminate behavior challenges for the student
7.   Ways to involve the student in different classroom activities in all subject areas (e.g., math, English, science) and instruction strategies (e.g., small-group work, lectures, individual work)
8.   Descriptions of how projects are modified or adapted so that the student can be successful
9.   A portfolio of the student's work including the original class assignment and a description of any adaptations or modifications
10.  Tips on involving the student with her or his peers—that is, understanding how the student communicates
11.  Names of friends or particular individuals with whom the student has a relationship to schedule classes with for the next

year (A photograph or brief videotape of the student interacting and participating with other students and being supported successfully is a good complement to this part of the transition book.)

12.  Unique environmental arrangements that help support the student and other unique supports or dimensions of the student's support plan—for example, seating and positioning needs, personal care details, noise-level tolerance, and climate comfort levels

13.  Descriptions of the sending team's planning processes—that is, when they met, how they communicated and collaborated (For example, some teams meet weekly for 20 minutes and have a standard agenda. Often teams include the roles that different people assume to support this student. Although the receiving team may want to work differently, they report that it is helpful to understand the routines of the previous team.)

14.  Description of any equipment, communication devices, or other assistive technology that a student uses and how they are obtained, used, stored, transferred, and so forth, as well as the names of resource people in this area

Transition booklets should not be the only, or the primary, mode for transferring information about a child from a sending team to a receiving team. In addition, this information resource should **not**

1.  Be a list of the student's problems, troubles, or weaknesses
2.  Contain descriptors that could limit opportunities for this student or discourage people from getting to know the student directly
3.  Be a vehicle for others to think that they know or understand the student just because they have read the booklet

## CONCLUSIONS

It appears to be human nature that when things are going well, people forget to notice what is happening around them. Most often, when students are doing well in school, no one writes down the things that are happening because the supports become second nature. People assume that what they have discovered works well will continue to work well. These strategies are often the critical details that families and sending teams assume will be in place for the next school year.

Articulating what does work as a profile for the new group to use as a beginning place can be a very important step in ensuring that the student will be successful. Being deliberate about transition can go a long way toward ensuring the success of the student, the teams, and the school as new practices in ways of educating students are implemented. Not tapping the knowledge, experience, and expertise of people who know and support the student well is a seriously wasted resource.

# References

Action Council on Minority Education. (1990). *Education that works: An action plan for the education of minorities.* Cambridge: Massachusetts Institute of Technology, Quality Education for Minorities Project.

Allen, D. (1995). *The tuning protocol: A process for reflection.* Providence, RI: Coalition of Essential Schools.

Bagg-Rizzo, E. (1996). *A portrait of an individual moving through the special education continuum.* Unpublished master's thesis, San Diego State University, San Diego, CA.

Bandura, A. (1997). *Self-efficacy: The exercise of control.* New York: W.H. Freeman.

Barron, A. [Director], King, C., & Barron, A. [Producers]. (1984). *The shame of a nation* [Film]. New York: King Arthur Productions.

Baruth, L.G., & Manning, M.L. (1991). *Multicultural counseling and psychotherapy: A lifespan perspective.* Upper Saddle River, NJ: Merrill.

Baumgart, D., Brown, L., Pumpian, I., Nisbet, J.A., Ford, A., Sweet, M., Ranieri, L., Hansen, L., & Schroeder, J. (1980). The principle of partial participation and individualized adaptations in educational programs for severely handicapped students. In L. Brown, M.A. Falvey, I. Pumpian, D. Baumgart, J.A. Nisbet, A. Ford, J. Schroeder, & R. Loomis (Eds.), *Curricular strategies for teaching severely handicapped students functional skills in school and non-school environments* (Vol. X, pp. 152–205). Madison, WI: Madison Metropolitan School District.

Bergquist, W.H. (1993). *The postmodern organization: Mastering the art of irreversible change.* San Francisco: Jossey-Bass.

Berliner, D., & Biddle, B. (1996). Standards amidst uncertainty and inequality. *School Administrator, 53*(5), 42–47.

Blackorby, J., & Wagner, M. (1996). Longitudinal postschool outcomes of youth with disabilities: Findings from the National Longitudinal Transition Study. *Exceptional Children, 62,* 399–413.

Bos, C.S. (1995). Professional development and teacher change: Encouraging news from the trenches. *Remedial and Special Education, 16,* 379–382.

Brown, L., Nietupski, J., & Hamre-Nietupski, S. (1976). The criterion of ultimate functioning and public school services for severely handicapped children. In M.A. Thomas (Ed.), *Hey, don't forget about me! Education's investment in the severely, profoundly, and multiply handicapped: A report* (pp. 2–15). Reston, VA: Council for Exceptional Children.

Caine, R.N., & Caine, G. (1997). *Education on the edge of possibility.* Alexandria, VA: Association for Supervision and Curriculum Development.

Calculator, S.N., & Jorgensen, C.M. (Eds.). (1994). *Including students with severe disabilities in schools: Fostering communication, interaction, and participation.* San Diego: Singular Publishing Group.

California High School Task Force. (1992). *Second to none: A vision of the new California high school: The report of the California High School Task Force.* Sacramento: California State Department of Education.

Canady, R.L., & Rettig, M.D. (1995). *Block scheduling: A catalyst for change in high schools.* Princeton, NJ: Eye on Education.

Capra, F. (1994, Summer/Fall). From the parts to the whole: Systems thinking in ecology and education. *Elmwood Quarterly,* 31–37.

Carnine, D. (1997). Bridging the research-to-practice gap. *Exceptional Children, 63,* 513–521.

Castagnera, E., Fisher, D., Rodifer, K., & Sax, C. (1998). *Deciding what to teach and how to teach it: Connecting students through curriculum and instruction.* Colorado Springs, CO: PEAK.

Cawelti, G. (1997). *Effects of high school restructuring: Ten schools at work.* Arlington, VA: Educational Research Service.

Christ, G.M. (1995). Curriculums with real-world connections. *Educational Leadership, 52*(8), 32–35.

Cotton, K., & Savard, W. (1981). *Instructional grouping: Ability grouping* (Topic Summary Report, Research on School Effectiveness Project). Portland OR: Northwest Regional Educational Laboratory.

Council for Exceptional Children. (1998). State-wide assessment programs: Including students with disabilities. *Research Connections in Special Education, 2,* 1–8.

Cummins, J. (1989). *Empowering minority students.* Sacramento: California Association for Bilingual Education.

Darder, A. (1991). *Culture and power in the classroom: A critical foundation for bicultural education.* Westport, CT: Bergin & Garvey.

Deno, E. (1970). Special education as developmental capital. *Exceptional Children, 37*(3), 229–237.

Deshler, D.D. (1998). Grounding interventions for students with learning disabilities in "powerful ideas." *Learning Disabilities Research and Practice, 13*(1), 29–34.

Deshler, D.D., Ellis, E.S., & Lenz, B.K. (1996). *Teaching adolescents with learning disabilities: Strategies and methods* (2nd ed.). Denver: Love Publishing Co.

Dewey, J. (1916). *Democracy and education.* New York: Free Press.

Dobyns, L., & Crawford-Mason, C. (1994). *Thinking about quality: Progress, wisdom, and the Deming philosophy.* New York: Times Books.

Downing, J.E., Eichinger, J., & Williams, L.J. (1997). Comparative views of principals and educators at different levels of implementation. *Remedial and Special Education, 18,* 133–142.

Edgar, E. (1997). School reform, special education, and democracy. *Remedial and Special Education, 18,* 323–325.

Education for All Handicapped Children Act of 1975, PL 94-142, 20 U.S.C. §§ 1400 *et seq.*

England, R., Stewart, J., Jr., & Meier, K. (1990). Excellence in education: Second generation school discrimination as a barrier. *Equity and Excellence, 24*(4), 35–40.

Epstein, J.L. (1995). School/family/community partnerships: Caring for the children we share. *Phi Delta Kappan, 76*(9), 701–712.

Erickson, K.A., Koppenhaver, D.A., Yoder, D.E., & Nance, J. (1997). Integrating communication and literacy instruction for a child with multiple disabilities. *Focus on Autism and Other Developmental Disabilities, 12,* 142–150.

Erwin, E.J., & Soodak, L.C. (1995). I never knew I could stand up to the system: Families' perspectives on pursuing inclusive education. *Journal of The Association for Persons with Severe Handicaps, 20,* 136–146.

Evans, I.M., Salisbury, C., Palombaro, M., Berryman, J., & Hollowood, T. (1992). Peer interactions and social acceptance of elementary-age children with severe disabilities in an inclusive school. *Journal of The Association for Persons with Severe Handicaps, 17,* 205–212.

Evans, R. (1996). *The human side of school change: Reform, resistance, and the real-life problems of innovation.* San Francisco: Jossey-Bass.

Falvey, M.A. (1995). *Inclusive and heterogeneous schooling: Assessment, curriculum, and instruction.* Baltimore: Paul H. Brookes Publishing Co.

Featherstone, H. (1987). Organizing classes by ability. *Harvard Educational Letter, 3*(4), 1–4.

Feinberg, W., & Soltis, J.F. (1992). *Thinking about education series: School and society* (2nd ed.). New York: Teachers College Press.

Fisher, D. (1996). *Organizational climate, typical student attitudes, and parent satisfaction: A study of a traditional and an inclusive high school.* Unpublished doctoral dissertation, Claremont Graduate School and San Diego State University, San Diego, CA.

Fisher, D., Sax, C., & Jorgensen, C.M. (1998). Philosophical foundations of inclusive, restructuring schools. In C.M. Jorgensen, *Restructuring high schools for all students: Taking inclusion to the next level* (pp. 29–47). Baltimore: Paul H. Brookes Publishing Co.

Fisher, D., Sax, C., & Pumpian, I. (1996). From intrusion to inclusion: Myths and realities in our schools. *Reading Teacher, 49,* 580–584.

Fisher, D., Sax., C., Pumpian, I., Rodifer, K., & Kreikemeirer, P. (1997). Including all students in the high school reform agenda. *Education and Treatment of Children, 20,* 59–67.

Friedlander, H. (1995). *The origins of Nazi genocide: From euthanasia to the final solution.* Chapel Hill: University of North Carolina Press.

Fryxell, D., & Kennedy, C.H. (1995). Placement along the continuum of services and its impact on students' social relationships. *Journal of The Association for Persons with Severe Handicaps, 20,* 259–269.

Fullan, M. (1993). *School development and management series: Change forces: Probing the depth of educational reform.* New York: Falmer Press.

Fulton, K. (1993). Teaching matters: The role of technology in education. *Ed-Tech Review,* 5–10.

General Accounting Office. (1994, August). *Educational reform: School-based management results in changes in instruction and budgeting.* Washington, DC: Author.

George, P. (1988). *What's the truth about tracking and ability grouping really???* (Handout). Available from the University of Florida, Gainesville.

Giangreco, M.E., Dennis, R., Cloninger, C., Edelman, S., & Schattman, R. (1993). "I've counted Jon": Transformational experiences of teachers educating students with disabilities. *Exceptional Children, 59,* 359–372.

Gibb, G.S., Young, J.R., Allred, K.W., Dyches, T.T., Egan, M.W., & Ingram, C.F. (1997). A team-based junior high inclusion program. *Remedial and Special Education, 18,* 243–249.

Glickman, C.D. (1993). *Renewing America's schools: A guide for school-based action.* San Francisco: Jossey-Bass.

Glines, D. (1984). The future of global society. In A.M. Ochoa & J. Hurtado (Eds.), *Educational and societal futures: Meeting the technological demands of the 1990's* (pp. 22–31). San Diego: National Origin Desegregation Center.

Goals 2000: Educate America Act of 1994, PL 103-227, 20 U.S.C. §§ 5801 *et seq.*

Good, T., & Brophy, J. (1987). *Looking in classsrooms* (4th ed.). New York: HarperCollins.

Goodlad, J.I. (1984). *A place called school: Prospects for the future.* New York: McGraw-Hill.

Gronna, S., Jenkins, A., & Chin-Chance, S. (1998). Who are we assessing? Determining state-wide participation rates for students with disabilities. *Exceptional Children, 64,* 407–418.

Guralnick, M.J. (1994). Mothers' perceptions of the benefits and drawbacks of early childhood mainstreaming. *Journal of Early Intervention, 18,* 168–183.

Hanline, M.F. (1993). Inclusion of pre-schoolers with profound disabilities: An analysis of children's interactions. *Journal of The Association for Persons with Severe Handicaps, 18,* 28–35.

Hanson, M.J., & Lynch, E.W. (1992). Family diversity: Implications for policy and practice. *Topics in Early Childhood Special Education, 12,* 283–306.

Hatch, T. (1998). How comprehensive can comprehensive reform be? *Phi Delta Kappan, 79,* 518–522.

Hauser, J., & Malouf, D. (1996). A federal perspective on special education technology. *Journal of Learning Disabilities, 29,* 504–511.

Haycock, K., & Navarro, M.S. (1988). *Unfinished business: Fulfilling our children's promise.* Albany, NY: Achievement Council.

Heifetz, R.A. (1994). *Leadership without easy answers.* Cambridge, MA: Belknap Press.

Heward, W.L., & Orlansky, M.D. (1992). *Exceptional children: An introductory survey of special education* (4th ed.). Upper Saddle River, NJ: Merrill.

Hickman, C.W., Greenwood, G., & Miller, M.D. (1995). High school parent involvement: Relationships with achievement, grade level, SES, and gender. *Journal of Research and Development in Education, 28,* 125–133.

Higher Education Act, PL 89-329, 20 U.S.C. §§ 1001 *et seq.*

Hirsch, E.D., Jr. (1987). *Cultural literacy: What every American needs to know.* Boston: Houghton Mifflin.

Hitzing, W. (1980). ENCOR and beyond. In T. Appolloni, J. Cappuccilli, & T.P. Cooke (Eds.), *Achievements in residential services for persons with disabilities: Toward excellence* (pp. 24–40). Baltimore: University Park Press.

Hocutt, A.M. (1996). Effectiveness of special education: Is placement the critical factor? *The Future of Children: Special Education for Students with Disabilities, 6*(1), 77–102.

Hollowood, T.M., Salisbury, C.L., Rainforth, B., & Palombaro, M.M. (1994). Use of instructional time in classrooms serving students with and without severe disabilities. *Exceptional Children, 61,* 242–253.

Hunt, P., & Goetz, L. (1997). Research on inclusive educational programs, practices, and outcomes for students with severe disabilities. *Journal of Special Education, 31,* 3–29.

Hunt, P., Staub, D., Alwell, M., & Goetz, L. (1994). Achievement by all students within the context of cooperative learning groups. *Journal of The Association for Persons with Severe Handicaps, 19,* 290–301.

Improving America's Schools Act of 1994, PL 103-382, 20 U.S.C. §§ 6300 *et seq.*

Individuals with Disabilities Education Act (IDEA) Amendments of 1991, PL 102-119, 20 U.S.C. §§ 1400 *et seq.*

Individuals with Disabilities Education Act (IDEA) Amendments of 1997, PL 105-17, 20 U.S.C. §§ 1400 *et seq.*

Individuals with Disabilities Education Act (IDEA) of 1990, PL 101-476, 20 U.S.C. §§ 1400 *et seq.*

Jacobs, H.H. (1997). *Mapping the big picture: Integrating curriculum and assessment, K–12.* Alexandria, VA: Association for Supervision and Curriculum Development.

Janney, R.E., & Snell, M.E. (1996). How teachers use peer interactions to include students with moderate and severe disabilities in elementary general education classes. *Journal of The Association for Persons with Severe Handicaps, 21,* 72–80.

Jensen, E. (1998). *Teaching with the brain in mind.* Alexandria, VA: Association for Supervision and Curriculum Development.

Jorgensen, C.M. (1998). *Restructuring high schools for all students: Taking inclusion to the next level.* Baltimore: Paul H. Brookes Publishing Co.

Jorgensen, C.M., Fisher, D., Sax, C., & Skoglund, K.L. (1998). Innovative scheduling, new roles for teachers, and heterogeneous grouping: The organizational factors related to student success in inclusive, restructuring schools. In C.M. Jorgensen, *Restructuring high schools for all students: Taking inclusion to the next level* (pp. 49–70). Baltimore: Paul H. Brookes Publishing Co.

Jorgensen, C.M. [Director and Producer], Mroczka, M. [Producer], & Williams, S. [Producer]. (1999). *High school inclusion: Equity and excellence in an inclusive community of learners* [Videotape]. Baltimore: Paul H. Brookes Publishing Co.

Justen, J. (1976). Who are the severely handicapped? A problem of definition. *AAESPH Review, 1,* 1–11.

Kennedy, C.H., & Itkonen, T. (1994). Some effects of regular class participation on the social contacts and social networks of high school students with severe disabilities. *Journal of The Association for Persons with Severe Handicaps, 19,* 1–10.

Kostner, J. (1996). *Virtual leadership: Secrets from the round table for the multi-site manager.* New York: Warner Books.

Kuhmerker, L. (1992). Freedom and democracy at the Sudbury Valley School. *Moral Education Forum, 17*(4), 1–9.

Kulik, C., & Kulik, J. (1987). Effects of ability grouping on secondary school students: A meta-analysis of evaluation findings. *American Educational Research Journal, 19*(3), 415–428.

Kunc, N. (1992). The need to belong: Rediscovering Maslow's hierarchy of needs. In R.A. Villa, J.S. Thousand, W. Stainback, & S. Stainback (Eds.), *Restructuring for caring and effective education: An administrative guide to creating heterogeneous schools* (pp. 25–39). Baltimore: Paul H. Brookes Publishing Co.

Kunc, N. (1997, February). *Ridding ourselves of the habits of exclusion: What we have learned.* Keynote presentation at the Colorado Inclusion Conference, Denver.

Lara, J. (1994). Demographic overview: Changes in student enrollment in American schools. In K. Spangenberg-Urbschat & R. Pritchard (Eds.), *Kids come in all languages: Reading instruction for ESL students* (pp. 9–21). Newark, DE: International Reading Association.

Lipsky, D.K., & Gartner, A. (Eds.). (1997). *Inclusion and school reform: Transforming America's classrooms.* Baltimore: Paul H. Brookes Publishing Co.

Lutfiyya, Z.M. (1988). *Materials on relationships.* Syracuse, NY: Syracuse University, Center on Human Policy. (ERIC Document Reproduction Service No. ED 307 738)

Mackin, R. (1997, October). *Creating an inclusive, restructured high school.* Keynote address at the Equity and Excellence Conference, Portsmouth, NH.

Marsal, L. (1998, February/March). CEC launches initiative on special education teaching conditions. *CEC Today, 2.*

Massachusetts Institute of Technology, Quality Education for Minorities Project. (1990). *Education that works: An action plan for the education of minorities.* Cambridge: Author.

Massell, D., Kirst, M., & Hoppe, M. (1997, March). *Persistence and change: Standards-based systemic reform in nine states* (CPRE Policy Brief). Philadelphia: University of Pennsylvania.

Mather, N. (1998). Dr. Samuel A. Kirk: The complete professor. *Learning Disabilities Research and Practice, 13*(1), 35–42.

McAnaney, K.D. (1992). *I wish: Dreams and realities of parenting a special needs child.* Sacramento: United Cerebral Palsy Association of California.

McDonnell, J.J., Hardman, M.L., McDonnell, A.P., & Kiefer-

O'Donnell, R. (1995). *An introduction to persons with severe disabilities.* Needham Heights, MA: Allyn & Bacon.

McDonnell, L., & McLaughlin, M. (Eds.). (1997). *Educating one and all: Students with disabilities and standards-based reform.* Washington, DC: National Academy Press.

McGregor, G., & Volgelsberg, R.T. (1998). *Inclusive schooling practices: Pedagogical and research foundations.* Pittsburgh: Allegheny University of the Health Sciences.

McLaughlin, M., & Verstegen, D. (1998). Increasing regulatory flexibility of special education programs: Problems and promising strategies. *Exceptional Children, 64,* 371–384.

Meyer, L.H., Park, H.-S., Grenot-Scheyer, M., Schwartz, I.S., & Harry, B. (Eds.). (1998). *Making friends: The influences of culture and development.* Baltimore: Paul H. Brookes Publishing Co.

Meyer, L.H., Peck, C.A., & Brown, L. (Eds.). (1991). *Critical issues in the lives of people with severe disabilities.* Baltimore: Paul H. Brookes Publishing Co.

Miles, K.H. (1995). Freeing resources for improving schools: A case study of teacher allocation in Boston public schools. *Educational Evaluation and Policy Analysis, 17,* 476–493.

Miller, R.J., Strain, P.S., Boyd, K., Hunsiker, S., McKinley, J., & Wu, A. (1992). Parents' attitudes toward integration. *Topics in Early Childhood Education, 12,* 230–246.

National Association of State Boards of Education (NASBE). (1992). *Winners all: A call for inclusive schools.* Alexandria, VA: Author.

National Association of State Boards of Education (NASBE) Study Group on Special Education. (1995). *Winning ways: Creating inclusive schools, classrooms, and communities.* Alexandria, VA: Author.

National Commission on Excellence in Education. (1983). *A nation at risk: The imperative for educational reform.* Washington, DC: U.S. Government Printing Office.

National Commission on Teaching and America's Future (NCTAF). (1996). *What matters most: Teaching for America's future: Report of the National Commission on Teaching and America's Future.* New York: Author.

Nieto, S. (1996). *Affirming diversity: The sociopolitical context of multicultural education* (2nd ed.). White Plains, NY: Addison Wesley Longman.

Oakes, J. (1985). *Keeping track: How schools structure inequality.* New Haven, CT: Yale University Press.

Oakes, J., & Lipton, M. (1990). *Making the best of schools: A handbook for parents, teachers, and policymakers.* New Haven, CT: Yale University Press.

Oakes, J., & Wells, A. (1998). Detracking for high student achievement. *Education Leadership, 55*(6), 38–41.

Ochoa, A.M., & Romo, H. (1977). *Lau Center manual IV recommendations and framework for developing a comprehensive educational master plan to comply with Title VI or the CRA 1964.* San Diego: National Origin Desegregation Center.

Olson, L. (1994, May 4). Critical friends. *Education Week,* 20–27.

Onosko, J.J., & Jorgensen, C. (1998). Unit and lesson planning in the inclusive classroom: Maximizing learning opportunities for all students. In C.M. Jorgensen, *Restructuring high schools for all students: Taking inclusion to the next level* (pp. 71–105). Baltimore: Paul H. Brookes Publishing Co.

Patterson, J.L., Purkey, S.C., & Parker, J.V. (1986). *Productive school systems for a nonrational world.* Alexandria, VA: Association for Supervision and Curriculum Development.

Perske, R. (1993). Introduction. In A.N. Amado (Ed.), *Friendships and community connections between people with and without developmental disabilities* (pp. 1–6). Baltimore: Paul H. Brookes Publishing Co.

Phelps, A., & Hanley-Maxwell, C. (1997). School-to-work transitions for youth with disabilities: A review of outcomes and practices. *Review of Educational Research, 67,* 197–226.

Pimentel, R. (1981). *Windmills attitudinal training program.* Sacramento: California Governor's Council on the Employment of the Handicapped.

Postman, N. (1985). *Amusing ourselves to death: Public discourse in the age of show business.* New York: Viking Press.

Putnam, J.W. (1998). *Cooperative learning and strategies for inclusion: Celebrating diversity in the classroom* (2nd ed.). Baltimore: Paul H. Brookes Publishing Co.

Rist, R. (1970). Social class and teacher expectations: The self-fulfilling prophecy in ghetto education. *Harvard Education Review, 49,* 411–451.

Roach, V. (1991). Special education: New questions in an era of reform. *State Board Connection, 11*(6), 1–7.

Roach, V., Fisher, D., & McGregor, G. (1996, December). A framework for evaluating state and local policies for inclusion. *CISP Issue Brief, 1*(1), 1–9.

Roach, V., Halvorsen, A., Zeph, L., Giugno, M., & Caruso, M. (1997). Providing accurate placement data on students with disabilities in general education settings. *CISP Issue Brief, 2*(3), 1–9.

Rodifer, K. (1997). *Teachers' perceptions of supports and resources in an inclusive high school.* Unpublished master's thesis, San Diego State University, San Diego, CA.

Roosevelt, F.D. (1945). Undelivered address prepared for Jefferson Day to be delivered April 13, 1945. In National Park Service, *His words: Franklin Delano Roosevelt*. Washington, DC: U.S. Government Printing Office.

Rosenbaum, J. (1976). *Making inequality: The hidden curriculum of high school tracking*. New York: John Wiley & Sons.

Rosenstock, L. (1997, November). *Onward through the fog: Where have we come from and where are we going?* Paper presented at the San Diego School-to-Career Conference.

Rowan, B., & Miracle, A. (1983). Systems of ability grouping and the stratification of achievement in elementary schools. *Sociology of Education, 26*(3), 133–144.

*Rules of the road*. (n.d.). Amherst, NH: Jefferson High School.

Ryndak, D.L., Downing, J.E., Jacqueline, L.R., & Morrison, A.P. (1995). Parents' perceptions after inclusion of their children with moderate or severe disabilities. *Journal of The Association for Persons with Severe Handicaps, 20,* 147–157.

Sagor, R. (1991, March). What Project LEARN reveals about collaborative action research. *Educational Leadership,* 6–10.

Sailor, W. (1991). Special education in the restructured school. *Remedial and Special Education, 12*(6), 8–22.

Salisbury, C. (1992). Parents as team members: Inclusive teams, collaborative outcomes. In B. Rainforth, J. York, & C. Macdonald (Eds.), *Collaborative teams for students with severe disabilities: Integrating therapy and educational services* (pp. 43–66). Baltimore: Paul H. Brookes Publishing Co.

Salisbury, C.L., Palombaro, M.M., & Hollowood, T.M. (1993). On the nature and change of an inclusive elementary school. *Journal of The Association for Persons with Severe Handicaps, 18,* 75–84.

Sautter, R.C. (1994). Who are today's city kids? Beyond the deficit model. *Cityschools, 1*(1), 6–10.

Schaefer, W., & Olexa, C. (1971). *Tracking and opportunity: The locking out process and beyond*. Scranton, PA: Chandler Press.

Schalock, M., Fredericks, B., Dalke, B., & Alberto, P. (1994). The house that TRACES built: A conceptual model of service delivery systems and implications for change. *Journal of Special Education, 28*(2), 203–223.

Schlechty, P.C. (1997). *Inventing better schools: An action plan for educational reform*. San Francisco: Jossey-Bass.

Schnorr, R.F. (1997). From enrollment to membership: "Belonging" in middle and high school classes. *Journal of The Association for Persons with Severe Handicaps, 22,* 1–15.

School-to-Work Opportunity Act of 1994, PL 103-239, 20 U.S.C. §§ 6101 *et seq.*

Schorr, L.B. (1997). *Common purpose: Strengthening families and neighborhoods to rebuild America.* New York: Anchor/Doubleday.

Secretary's Commission on Achieving Necessary Skills (SCANS). (1992). *Learning a living: A blueprint for high performance.* Washington, DC: U.S. Department of Labor.

Senge, P.M. (1990). *The fifth discipline: The art and practice of the learning organization.* New York: Doubleday/Currency.

Sergiovanni, T.J. (1994). *Building community in schools.* San Francisco: Jossey-Bass.

Sergiovanni, T.J. (1996). *Leadership for the schoolhouse: How is it different? Why is it important?* San Francisco: Jossey-Bass.

Servatius, J., Fellows, M., & Kelly, D. (1989). *Schools are for all kids: The leadership challenge.* Unpublished training manual, San Francisco State University, California Research Institute, San Francisco, CA.

Sharpe, M.N., York, J.L., & Knight, J. (1994). Effects of inclusion on the academic performance of classmates without disabilities: A preliminary study. *Remedial and Special Education, 15,* 281–287.

Showers, B., Joyce, B., Scanlon, M., & Schnaubelt, C. (1998). A second chance to read. *Educational Leadership, 55*(6), 27–30.

Siegel, P.M., & Byrne, S. (1994). *Using quality to redesign school systems: The cutting edge of common sense.* San Francisco: Jossey-Bass.

Sizer, T. (1989). Diverse practice, shared ideas: The essential school. In H. Walberg & J. Lane (Eds.), *Organizing for learning: Toward the 21st century* (pp. 1–8). Reston, VA: National Association of Secondary School Principals.

Sizer, T.R. (1992). *Horace's compromise: The dilemma of the American high school.* Boston: Houghton Mifflin.

Slavin, R. (1987). Ability grouping and student achievement in elementary grades: A best-evidence synthesis. *Review of Educational Research, 57*(3), 293–336.

Slavin, R.E., & Braddock, J.H. (1994). Ability grouping: On the wrong track. In J.I. Goodlad & P. Keating (Eds.), *Access to knowledge: The continuing agenda for our nation's schools* (pp. 289–296). New York: College Entrance Examination Board.

Smith, G.J., Edelen-Smith, P.J., & Stodden, R.A. (1998). Effective practice for generating outcomes of significance: The complexities of transformational change. In A. Hilton & R. Ringlaben (Eds.), *Best and promising practices in developmental disabilities* (pp. 331–342). Austin, TX: PRO-ED.

Smith, M., & O'Day, J. (1991). Systemic school reform. In S.H.

Fuhrman & B. Malen (Eds.), *The politics of curriculum and testing* (pp. 223–267). New York: Falmer Press.

Smyth, J. (Ed.). (1989). *Deakin studies in education series: Critical perspectives on educational leadership.* New York: Falmer Press.

Sorenson, A., & Hallinan, M. (1986). Effects of ability grouping on growth in academic achievement. *American Educational Research Journal, 23,* 519–542.

Sparks, D., & Hirsh, S. (1997). *A new vision for staff development.* Alexandria VA: Association for Supervision and Curriculum Development.

SRI International. (1990). *National longitudinal transition study of special education students.* Menlo Park, CA: Author.

Stainback, S., Stainback, W., & Forest, M. (Eds.). (1989). *Educating all students in the mainstream of regular education.* Baltimore: Paul H. Brookes Publishing Co.

Staub, D., Schwartz, I.S., Gallucci, C., & Peck, C.A. (1994). Four portraits of friendships at an inclusive school. *Journal of The Association for Persons with Severe Handicaps, 19,* 314–325.

Steinbeck, J. (1938). *Of mice and men.* New York: The Modern Library.

Steinbeck, J. (1947). *The pearl.* New York: Viking Press.

Stevens, R.J., & Slavin, R.E. (1995). The cooperative elementary school: Effects on students' achievement, attitudes, and social relations. *American Educational Research Journal, 32,* 321–351.

Stolovitch, H.D., & Lane, M. (1989). Multicultural training: Designing for affective results. *Performance & Instruction, 28,* 10–15.

Stringer, E.T. (1996). *Action research: A handbook for practitioners.* Thousand Oaks, CA: Sage Publications.

Strully, J.L., & Strully, C.F. (1989). Family support to promote integration. In S. Stainback, W. Stainback, & M. Forest (Eds.), *Educating all students in the mainstream of regular education* (pp. 213–219). Baltimore: Paul H. Brookes Publishing Co.

Tally, S., & Martinez, D.H. (1998). *Tools for schools: School reform models supported by the National Institute on the Education of At Risk Students.* Washington, DC: U.S. Department of Education, Office of Education Research and Improvement.

Thousand, J.S., & Villa, R.A. (1992). Collaborative teams: A powerful tool in school restructuring. In R.A. Villa, J.S. Thousand, W. Stainback, & S. Stainback (Eds.), *Restructuring for caring and effective education: An administrative guide to creating heterogeneous schools* (pp. 73–108). Baltimore: Paul H. Brookes Publishing Co.

Tomlinson, C.A. (1995). *How to differentiate instruction in mixed-ability classrooms.* Alexandria, VA: Association for Supervision and Curriculum Development.

Trotter, A. (1997, November 10). Taking technology's measure. In Technology counts: Schools and reform in the information age. *Education Week, 17*(11), 6–11.

Tucker, C.M., Chennault, S.A., Brady, B.A., Fraser, K.P., Gaskin, V.T., Dunn, C., & Frisby, C. (1995). A parent, community, public schools, and university involved partnership education program to examine and boost academic achievement and adaptive functioning skills of African-American students. *Journal of Research and Development in Education, 28,* 174–185.

Tucker, M.S., & Codding, J.B. (1998). *Standards for our schools: How to set them, measure them, and reach them.* San Francisco: Jossey-Bass.

Turnbull, A.P., & Broniki, G.J. (1986). Changing second grader's attitudes toward people with mental retardation: Using kid power. *Mental Retardation, 24,* 44–45.

Turnbull, A.P., & Turnbull, H.R., III. (1997). *Families, professionals, and exceptionality: A special partnership* (3rd ed.). Upper Saddle River, NJ: Merrill.

U.S. Department of Education. (1995). *Seventeenth annual report to Congress on the implementation of the Individuals with Disabilities Education Act.* Washington, DC: Author.

U.S. Department of Education. (1996). What is a schoolwide program? In *Improving America's schools: A newsletter on issues in school reform.* Washington, DC: Author.

U.S. Department of Education. (1998). *Title V of the Higher Education Act: U.S. Department of Education's proposal for reauthorization.* Unpublished paper, U.S. Department of Education, Office of the Secretary of Education.

U.S. General Accounting Office, Health, Education, and Human Services Division. (1994, August). *Educational reform: School-based management results in changes in instruction and budgeting: Report to Congressional requesters.* Washington, DC: Author.

Vanderwood, M., McGrew, K., & Ysseldyke, J. (1998). Why we can't say much about students with disabilities during educational reform. *Exceptional Children, 63,* 359–370.

Vanfossen, B., Jones, J., & Spade, J. (1987). Curriculum tracking and status maintenance. *Sociology of Education, 60,* 104–122.

Vaughn, S., Schumm, J., & Brick, J. (1998). Using a rating scale to design and evaluate inclusion programs. *Teaching Exceptional Children, 30*(4), 41–45.

Villa, R.A., & Thousand, J.S. (1992). Restructuring public school systems: Strategies for organizational change and progress. In R.A. Villa, J.S. Thousand, W. Stainback, & S. Stainback (Eds.), *Restructuring for caring and effective education: An administrative guide to creating heterogeneous schools* (pp. 109–137). Baltimore: Paul H. Brookes Publishing Co.

Villa, R.A., Thousand, J.S., Stainback, W., & Stainback, S. (Eds.). (1992). *Restructuring for caring and effective education: An administrative guide to creating heterogeneous schools.* Baltimore: Paul H. Brookes Publishing Co.

Wagner, M. (1993). *The transition experiences of young people with disabilities. A summary of findings from the National Longitudinal Transition Study of Special Education Students.* Menlo Park, CA: SRI. (ERIC Document Reproduction Service No. EC302815)

Wagner, M., & Blackorby, J. (1996). Transition from high school to work or college: How special education students fare. *The Future of Children: Special Education for Students with Disabilities, 6*(1), 103–120.

Wagner, T. (1998). Change as collaborative inquiry: A "constructivist" methodology for reinventing schools. *Phi Delta Kappan, 79,* 512–517.

Waldron, N., & McLeskey, J. (1998). The effects of an inclusive school program on students with mild and severe learning disabilities. *Exceptional Children, 64,* 395–405.

Wang, M.C. (1988, May 4). A "promising approach" for reforming special education: Commentary. *Education Week, 36,* 28.

Warner, M., Cheney, C., & Pienkowski, D. (1996). Guidelines for developing and evaluating programs for secondary students with mild disabilities. *Intervention in School and Clinic, 31,* 276–284.

Weisendanger, K., & Birlen, E. (1981). A critical look at the reading approaches and grouping currently used in the primary grades. *Reading Horizons, 22*(1), 54–58.

Wheatley, M.J., & Kellner-Rogers, M. (1996). *A simpler way.* San Francisco: Berrett-Koehler.

Wheelock, A. (1992). *Crossing the tracks: How untracking can save America's schools.* New York: New Press.

Wilson, C., & Wright, L. (1994). Enhancing access to knowledge through school and district organization. In J.I. Goodlad & P. Keating (Eds.), *Access to knowledge: The continuing agenda for our nation's schools* (pp. 223–224). New York: College Entrance Examination Board.

Wilson, K.G., & Daviss, B. (1996). *Redesigning education.* New York: Teachers College Press.

Wohlstetter, P., Smyer, R., & Mohrman, S.A. (1994). New boundaries for school based management: The high involvement model. *Educational Evaluation and Policy Analysis, 16,* 268–286.

Wolfensberger, W. (1972). *Normalization: The principle of normalization in human services.* Toronto: National Institute on Mental Retardation.

York, J., & Tundidor, M. (1995). Issues raised in the name of inclusion: Perspectives of educators, parents, and students. *Journal of The Association for Persons with Severe Handicaps, 20,* 31–44.

Zipper, I.N., Hinton, C., Weil, M., & Rounds, K. (1993). *Service coordination for early intervention: Parents and professionals.* Cambridge, MA: Brookline Books.

# Index

*Page numbers followed by "f" indicate figures; those followed by "t" indicate tables.*

## DATE DUE